This book is dedicated to:

All the former pupils of the; Yoredale and Richmond Grammar Schools, who fought for freedom and gave their lives in two World Wars.

Acknowledgements

I would like to thank the following for their help and contributions in the compiling of this story. All gave freely of their time and many loaned precious photographs with no time laid for their return.

George Broadley (Photographs and family background) brother to Alan, Ernest Adams, cousin, Sylvia Coates cousin (Loan of a facsimile of Alan's flying logbook) Terry Wray cousin and school friend who's description of his schooldays with Alan was crucial. David Squires former Richmond Grammar School pupil (photographs and Grammar School 'Compostellan' information) Mike Proctor Richmondshire historian, Norman Didwell Flight Mechanic 99 Squadron, Brian Alderson and the many people of Richmond and Leyburn who offered advice and help.

The staff at the Public Record Office, Kew.

Finally a very special thank you to Kitty Jeffery (Nee Ovesby) for her very personal contribution.

A.E.E.

CONTENTS

FROM THE DALES
To
JERICHO

The story of Alan Broadley
DSO DFC DFM

By
A.E.Eaton.

ISBN 0 9536331 0 1

Published by
Recall Publications
50,Turker Lane
Northallerton
North Yorks. DL6 1QA

Chapter One

Schooldays

Close to the green and undulating landscape of the Yorkshire Dales, lies the quiet North Yorkshire market town of Leyburn. In the Market Square at the centre of the town, stands a Memorial Cross to the memory of the local men who laid down their lives in two World Wars. Although each one of those men named on that simple stone cross is remembered with great pride and sadness, there is one name that stands out as the epitome of bravery and duty. That name is John Alan Broadley. DSO DFC DFM The story of this airman is one of courage and determination through more than four years of distinguished operational flying in Europe during World War11. On qualifying as an Air Observer and serving with Bomber Command in the early days of the war, Alan Broadley became involved in some of the most dangerous and secretive operations with the Special Operations Executive (SOE) and Special Duties Squadrons. He was then posted to a Mosquito squadron and flew on many raids against rocket installations in occupied Europe, culminating in 'Operation Jericho' the spectacular low level Mosquito attack on the Gestapo controlled prison at Amiens, to release French patriots.
This is the story of that young Dalesman.

***

Alan Broadley (he preferred the second of his Christian names) was born in Leyburn on the 8th of February 1921 and was the son of Tom and Irene Broadley and younger brother to Anne. At the time of Alan's birth, his father with his brother John ran the family butcher's shop in the town centre. Tom also owned a market meat stall at the nearby town of Richmond, which he attended on market days. Sadly, within a few days of giving birth to her son, Mrs Broadley died and was laid to rest in the churchyard of Bellerby, a small village but few miles from Leyburn. With the loss of his wife and mother of his two children, Tom Broadley found great difficulty in running a business and raising two young children. To ensure that they had the shelter of a warm and loving household, arrangements were made for them to live with their maternal grandmother, Mrs R. Adamson who lived at St. Mary's Mount Leyburn. This arrangement of fostering worked very well and the two toddlers soon settled into their new home. During the time Alan was living with his grandmother, he was often looked after by Ernest Adamson an older cousin of a dozen years and also by Ernest's sister Sylvia. Apart from being a companion and helping Alan to grow up, it sometimes fell to the young Ernest to wheel the baby Alan in his pram out through the streets of Leyburn. Mr Adamson who is now in his 91st year remembers it all with a great deal of affection and pride, but at the time found it somewhat of a chore. Alan and Anne lived with their grandmother for almost three years, but as they neared school age, a Nurse Marion MacDonald, who hailed from Liverpool, was employed to take charge of them. Later they were sent to live with their Aunt Peggy a younger sister of Alan's father. The reason for the move was due to Sylvia Adamson contracting scarlet fever and it was thought wise to move the two youngsters away. Aunt Peggy lived and worked above the family butcher's shop in Leyburn, which was owned by William Broadley, the patriarch of the Broadley family. Her job at the shop was to keep the books and generally help at the counter. Peggy was unmarried at this time but later married Jack Siddall the proprietor of the radio and electrical shop in the town. Jack Siddall bought and converted a nearby property into a shop cum house in which he, Peggy, Mr William Broadley and the two youngsters went to live. Jack and Peggy remained childless throughout their marriage but looked after the two infants as if they were their own. Despite the upheaval in their lives, the two children thrived and became very fond of their new 'parents'. During the time of their fostering, Tom Broadley carried on with his butchery business, dividing his time between Richmond and Leyburn. When working at Richmond, he often frequented the Fleece Hotel in the centre of the town. It was there he met the landlady of the hotel, widow, Ada Kitchen. Their friendship blossomed and they married a short time later.

Alan and Anne's early schooling was at the County Council Primary School in Leyburn, one of the small council run schools in the area. One companion at the primary school was their cousin and close friend, James Wray who bore the name Broadley as his second Christian name. Jimmy remembers that both he and Alan were sent to school with a pocket watch pinned to their woolly jerseys, but he cannot remember why as neither of them could tell the time. In the summer of 1931 Alan and Jimmy transferred to the Yorebridge Grammar School, situated between the villages of Askrigg and Bainbridge. (A school, no longer) It was here that Alan won a county minor scholarship that was to stand him in good stead in later years. At Yorebridge, Jimmy and other school friends gave Alan the nickname 'Butch' Broadley due to his family being in the butchery business. Jimmy recalls the good times Alan and he shared while they both were at Yorebridge School and in later years. There was always a friendly rivalry between the two of them, each striving to outdo the other at anything and everything. Alan learned to whistle through his fingers, a piercing whistle as Jimmy recalls, but Jimmy could never quite manage to do it. Jimmy could play the mouth organ better than Alan, and together they learned to yodel in the style, or so they thought, of Tex Ritter and Jimmy Van Huesen, two well known singers on the radio in those pre-war days. While at school, Alan introduced Jimmy to the dubious thrills of illicit smoking, a habit that was to get the young Broadley into trouble on more than one occasion. With their pooled weekly pocket money of tuppence, they would buy five Woodbines to share. If either the money or Woodbines ran out, which was often the case, they would try to smoke dried grass or any other such natural combustible materials. However Jimmy could never get away with smoking as it made him feel giddy and nauseous. Trouble loomed one day in school when they were attending woodwork class. Alan and Jimmy with some of the other boys sneaked out to the toilets to have a quick smoke. The woodwork teacher soon discovered their illegal activity and reported them to the headmaster. The Headmaster, Mr. R.C. Shorter, (who, in the time honoured humour of all schoolboys, was known as 'Arsy') decided to make an example of them all. Alan and the rest were hauled in front of him for interrogation and a reading of the 'riot act'. He asked those who had been caught smoking to take one step forward, by which time he was livid with anger. He strode along the line of boys and then without warning struck Alan a heavy blow on the side of the head with his hand, causing Alan to stagger somewhat, but somehow he managed to keep his feet. Alan told Jimmy later that he thought the Head had given him the clout because he hadn't been showing enough contrition. It appears that he had received the physical punishment for the entire group, and it had a very sobering effect on each one of them. As further punishment for their 'quick drag' break, the whole class was suspended from woodwork lessons and put to work making 200 paper cigarettes by cutting and winding paper round a pencil and securing the completed tubes with a spot of glue. A most laborious task. This finally stopped Jimmy from smoking, but he wasn't so sure it stopped Alan. Another pastime for the two of them was rat shooting 'safaris'. Each of them owned a .22in air rifle and they would climb onto the roof of the out buildings at the rear of the butcher's shop where there was the usual 'bone house' full of unwanted bones from the shop awaiting collection. There they would sit and wait to take pot shots at the scuttling scavenging rats nosing around the yard. Alan being a natural marksman was always more successful than Jimmy.

In mid 1934 at the age of thirteen, Alan left Leyburn and went to live with his father and at the same time left Yorebridge and transferred to Richmond Grammar School. His father had by now taken on the running of the Fleece Hotel with his wife and so it was decided to bring Alan back 'home' Anne was allowed to stay with Aunt Peggy. Although his home was in Richmond, Alan's heart was in Leyburn and he spent as much of his time there as possible, living in Richmond during the week and then travelling to Leyburn for weekends and holidays. With spending so much of his early life in Leyburn, he had developed a deep and lasting affection for the town and its people and grew to love that part of the Dales. Although Jimmy and he now went to different schools, they still met up at regular intervals at their local haunts in Leyburn, which naturally included the cinema. To earn extra pocket money they would often help out at the butcher's shop and one of the tasks they were sometimes given was to bring back a couple of bullocks for slaughter from a local farm. The pair of them would be dropped off at the farm, which was owned by a Mr. Tom Fall in the nearby village of Spennithorne. After collecting the bullocks they would drive them along the winding road back to Leyburn. It was reasonably safe to do so as the traffic was almost non existent along country roads in those days. Sometimes the two of them would go rabbit hunting at Tom Hall's farm with their four/ten shotguns, which they had managed to acquire by trading in their .22 air rifles. Jimmy says that the pair of them would blast away at the first sign of a rabbit, and as a result, the rabbit would bolt down into burrow and stay there. So that would be the end of the hunt. They just didn't have the patience to wait for any more to reappear.

While Alan was living at the Fleece Hotel he became friendly with a group of retired army officers who regaled him with tales of their wartime adventures on the Western Front. Listening to those men was probably germane to Alan's desire for a military career and apparently talking to and knowing them was the only redeeming thing about living in that large impersonal hotel. In early 1936 Alan's father and stepmother moved from the Fleece Hotel and took up the running of the recently refurbished Terrace House Hotel, an attractive Georgian building on the edge of the town. (Terrace House is now a retirement Home) Terrace House had an abundance of spacious gardens and was free from the noise of traffic and the busy sounds of the town. Alan was more relaxed living there but he still preferred the life and the friendliness of Leyburn. It was about this time that romance came into the young Alan's life. The young girl who was to be part of his life was Kitty Ovesby, a 14-year old school girl who lived with her parents at Low Coalsgarth Farm a few miles from Richmond. Kitty attended the Richmond High School for Girls, which was some distance from the Grammar School. She and Alan met when they both were invited to a mutual friend's Christmas party, and by chance were seated opposite one another on the long supper table. As the young do, they fell into conversation and got to know each other's names, and when it came to the time for dancing, Alan asked Kitty for a dance and they danced every dance for the remainder of the evening. Their friendship blossomed and they began to meet regularly after school and go for walks or visit the local cinema. Kitty soon learned that the young Alan was a quiet and thoughtful boy who seemed to hold a strong inner self-confidence. After a short while they were both introduced to each other's families and that was the beginning of a deep and loving friendship. Kitty recalls how the Girl's High School at Richmond, which was quite separate from the boys' school, did not have a gymnasium or any facilities for physical training, so the girls were compelled to use the gymnasium near the Grammar School Boarding House. The girls would have to trail crocodile fashion through the streets of the town to attend PT lessons, lessons looked forward to by most of the girls. Boys and girls being what they are, had their own way of communicating with one another, but school romances were never secret for very long as everyone soon learnt who was going out with whom, and Kitty's friendship with Alan was no exception. On more than one occasion during lessons, Kitty would hear a teacher use the expression "broadly speaking" when describing a point to a subject or making a reference. She would blush and pretend not to notice the suppressed giggles and knowing glances of the other girls in her class.

As time passed, Alan was developing into a wide shouldered and rugged but yet quiet determined young man. Academically, his progress at Richmond Grammar School was recognised as being steady rather than spectacular, as is the average pupil. However he performed reasonably well at sport, and by the time he was sixteen, he had earned his school colours both for rugby and cricket. He was rather better at cricket than rugby and apparently was a good stock slow bowler (but tended at times to bowl a bit too short) He also batted with enough ability not to be classed as a 'rabbit'. Mr Dickinson the school physics master and cricket coach remembers with a certain amount of chagrin how Alan would have to be chased and cajoled to take an interest in the game and to play to his best. He recalls that on more than one occasion when Alan was fielding, usually in the point/gully area, he would stand with the languid air of someone who was not particularly interested or paying attention. Then quite unexpectedly, after a batsman had played a latish cut, Alan would, in a flash pick the ball cleanly out of the air with unerring skill. He eventually won his cricket colours for the 1937 season and played in many games for the school. In one particular game of that season he was in the XI that played a match against Middlesbrough High School. The result was less than satisfactory. Middlesbrough H. S. team was bowled out for 95 runs with Richmond hanging on with just one wicket to spare after scoring a paltry 62. Alan was one of the few in the Richmond team to come away with some honour by taking five wickets for twenty two runs and scoring six runs not out, in a drawn game. Captain of the Richmond cricket team was the head prefect and senior scholar Frank Pedley who also captained the school rugby team. (It was he who put in the reports in the school magazine Compostellan that Alan tended to bowl a bit too short) Despite this he was recognised as a useful member of the school team.

June 18th. R.S.Y. v. Middlesbrough H.S. Away. Drawn Game.

MIDDLESBROUGH H.S.		R.S.Y.	
Hatch b. Calvert	4	Pendlebury c. Peel b. Hatch	1
Cooper b. Pedley	1	Harrison b. Cooper	2
Petrie b. Pedley	0	Pedley c. Petrie b. Hatch ...	5
Cargill not out	42	Squires run out	1
Baker c. & b. Broadley ...	23	Calvert J. c. & b. Hatch ...	34
Fawcett c. Harrison b. Calvert	0	White b. Cooper	2
Stitt b. Broadley	0	Atkinson c. Little b. Cooper	0
Rose c. White b. Broadley ...	0	Bell b. Cooper	0
Hewson l.b.w. b. Broadley ...	1	McGregor c. Baker b. Hewson	3
Little c. Pedley b. Calvert ...	8	Sanderson not out	2
Peel c. McGregor b. Broadley	3	Broadley not out	6
Extras	13	Extras	6
Total	95	Total (for 9 wkts.)	62

Calvert 3 for 13. Broadley 5 for 22.

The cricket score card taken from the 'Compostellan'

Alan also had the ability to play rugby well, but as is the wont of many young men, his lack of enthusiasm occasionally outstripped his ability. A report by the school sports master in 'Compostellan' for the 1937-38 rugby season states;

'Allan Broadley possesses a remarkable pair of hands and a kick that he might use more. He pushes hard in the tight, but does not make full use of his weight in loose scrums. He does not yet play with enough vigour and determination.

It is worth mentioning that one member of Richmond G.S. Cricket XI and Rugby XV carried the illustrious name of J.S.E Rob-Roy McGregor

Along with cricket and rugby, Alan was also a first class rifle shot. Mr Dickinson recalls taking a group of the school cadets to the North Riding

Cadet Corps shooting competition, which was being held at Northallerton. Richmond Grammar School won the competition but not without some drama. Mr Dickinson noted that Alan Broadley was the outstanding shot of all the cadets taking part and chose him for a 'shoot off decider' in a tied result. Despite all the tension and excitement, Alan remained cool and steady and won the competition for Richmond. Was that steadfastness a portent for future?

Although life in the 1930s was pleasant in many ways, the effects of the depression was being felt in this part of the North Riding of Yorkshire as it was in almost every other part of the country. Work was no easier to find in the Dales than it was in the industrial towns and cities. The depression was a great problem for many, but just as ominous in those days, was the threat of war looming large over Europe once again, due to the rise of Nazi Germany in 1933. Despite limitations set for military spending, Germany had begun a vast rearmament programme. In 1935 the British Government responded to the German threat by ordering a huge increase in defence spending and a vast increase in recruitment for the three services and the building of scores of aerodromes. Although he did not know it, Alan Broadley and many like him were to be the generation that was to be directly affected by those dramatic and historic events. Shortly after his eighteenth birthday, Alan left school and considered working in a bank, this however, was a short-lived idea. From his very early teens had wanted to be a civil aviation pilot and never really had thoughts of doing much else. When he was small boy, his uncle Jack, who had served with the Royal Flying Corps in the Great War had regaled the young Alan with tales of daring and danger in France and Flanders. That coupled with tales by the resident army officers he met at the hotel stirred him even more into thinking of joining one of the three armed services. With his ambition to be a pilot and the call for men to join the RAF, Alan made up his mind. From then on, all he ever wanted to do was join the Royal Air Force and fly, and the life, as a bank teller could not replace this desire. In the April of 1939, Alan volunteered for the RAF and was accepted. When he finally received his joining papers to join, he was known as;

580819 Aircraftman 2nd Class. (AC2) Broadley. J.A.

For Kitty Ovesby, her emotions were mixed when Alan joined the air force. She was proud that he volunteered to serve his country, but desperately sad at his leaving. They promised faithfully to write as often as possible and that was that. There was no turning back for Alan. He left the girl he loved the protection of the Dales and his family and travelled to the RAF induction centre to begin his military service. On the day he was due to leave, Aunt

Peggy, Alan's surrogate mother gave him two St. Christopher Medallions. One medallion he was to wear around his neck and the other he was to attach to his aircraft when he eventually qualified to fly. Travelling to the RAF centre was the first step for Alan in what was to be a remarkable career with the Royal Air Force over the next five years. When he first joined the RAF, Kitty was still at school and it was then she realised that he was no longer a grammar schoolboy, but a young man in uniform. When Alan went away, Kitty kept up her studies to achieve her ambition to be a physical training teacher and sports mistress. All through his training and her schooling they kept in contact but both knew that life for them was never to be the same.

Chapter Two

Service Life

Life in the RAF began with Alan and several hundred other aspiring airmen being sent for a series of medical examinations, eye tests, maths and English exams and a whole variety of aptitude tests. Alan passed all of these with ease and so it was onto the next stage of his service career. However before he was allowed anywhere near an aeroplane, he, like every other RAF recruit, had to undergo a basic training course before going onto higher things. On arrival at Blackpool for his basic training or 'Square bashing' as it was called, the 'Sprog' airmen were introduced to service life and all the discipline and acceptance of orders that was to be expected of them. Life for all recruits is at first confusing, with sergeant and corporal drill instructors (DIs) bawling what seemed to be contradictory and incoherent orders at the bewildered 'erks. However it wasn't long before they got the drift of what those orders meant or what would be the consequences if they weren't obeyed almost immediately. Each airman was issued with the plethora of kit deemed necessary for a member of the RAF to do his duty, all of which had to be crammed into what seemed to be an undersized kit bag. After several weeks of polishing anything and everything, learning how to march, salute, carry out proficient rifle drill and present himself in a military fashion, Alan passed out more or less as a competent airman. On completion of his basic training, he was sent for aircrew acceptance tests. To Alan's deep disappointment he failed the selection for pilot but was selected to train as an Observer, which was the next best thing. Although never to be the captain, he was to be a vital link in the flying of the aircraft. The training was not so long as that for a pilot, but it was very intense and very exacting. He waited for the posting to navigation school that was to get him off the ground. On the last day of May 1939, Alan was posted to No 9 Flying Training School to begin his training as an Air Observer. The position of Air Observer in an aircraft appears to be a confusing title. The Observer crew position is taken from the days of the Royal Flying Corps during the Great War, and his job was to observe, that is to look out and direct the flight of the aeroplane. In the later years it was in many ways to become one of the most complicated of any crew position. The Observer in the modern RAF of the 1920s and 1930s was expected to navigate, carry out the bombing and also to act as the air gunner. This then was the aircrew position for which Alan was to train and fly. After two months of intense flying training chiefly carried out in the Avro Anson, a slow twin engined aircraft previously used in Coastal Command and communications, and long hours of classroom training, Alan passed the navigation exams with ease, passing the exams thus belying the notion that his academic ability was supposed to be less than acceptable. His maths must have been of a very high standard, as navigation is nothing if it is not mathematics. Alan not only qualified as an Air Observer (Navigation) but also qualified as an Air Gunner.

On the 31st of July he was awarded his flying badge, a winged 'O' brevet to be worn above the left breast pocket of his uniform. A proud moment indeed. With the award of his flying badge, Alan was also promoted to the rank of sergeant. So his promotion and award of the flying 'O' was the first step toward operational flying with the RAF. The next stage was yet more training and learning how to put into practice the whole variety of tasks that was expected of an Observer with Bomber Command. At the time of their graduation, Alan and his colleagues were acutely aware of the international tension and that war with Germany was a distinct possibility and knew that sooner or later the flying would be for real. From No 9 Flying Training School, the newly promoted Sergeant Broadley was posted to RAF Usworth in County Durham where he stayed for three weeks before being sent to his first training squadron. On the 27th of August he arrived at No 215 Bomber Squadron based at RAF Honington in Suffolk. The squadron was operating the stately if somewhat useless Handley Page Harrow, the last of the bi-plane bombers to enter service with the Royal Air force. War clouds were looming ever nearer and within a week of his arrival at Honington, war had been declared. As a result, the RAF constantly moved and relocated squadrons from one airfield to another and by the 10th of September Alan was on the move once more. The squadron pilots flew the graceful but patently obsolete Harrow bombers down to RAF Bramcote in Nottinghamshire, where they were taken off operations and relegated to the training role. No 215 Squadron crews then began converting to the Vickers Wellington. The Wellington was a twin engined medium bomber, which had been in action over German targets from the outset of the war. From the very beginning, it proved itself as a very robust and reliable aircraft. The geodetic construction of the fuselage allowed it to absorb a great deal of anti aircraft fire and cannon shell damage. Alan Broadley was to find this out at first hand in the coming months. While at Bramcote, Alan carried out eight training exercises on the Wellington as the squadron prepared for war. The training sorties consisted of formation flying, air firing, bombing and navigation.

Certificates of Qualification.

(to be filled in as appropriate)

47690. P/O.

CENTRAL DEPOSITORY JUL 1946 ROYAL AIR FORCE

1. This is to certify that 580819. Sgt. BROADLEY J. A.
has qualified as AIR OBSERVER (NAVIGATION)
with effect from 31/6/39 Sgd. [illegible] S/L
Date 27/7/39 Unit No. 9. E&RFTS

2. This is to certify that 580819 Sgt. BROADLEY, J. A.
has qualified as BOMB-AIMER and AIR GUNNER
with effect from 31/7/39 Sgd. [illegible] S/L
Date 31/7/39 Unit No. 2. A.O.S.

3. This is to certify that 580819 SGT. J.A. BROADLEY
has qualified as BOMBING LEADER
with effect from 27/1/41 Sgd. [illegible]
Date 12/2/41. Unit [illegible] School

BOMBING LEADER [illegible] No. 20 OPT. U. LOSSIEMOUTH

4. This is to certify that 47690 P/O BROADLEY
has qualified as ASTRO- NAVIGATOR
with effect from 30/9/41 Sgd. [illegible] F/L
Date 31/9/41 Unit 1419 FLT.

The qualification page from Alan's logbook.

On the 23rd they were on the move once more, this time to Bassingbourne in Cambridgeshire. There they had a brief respite of two months and the squadron managed to carry out regular training sorties. On the 30th of November he was posted No 214 Squadron at Feltwell in Lincolnshire.

Squadron life appeared to be turmoil intermingled with chaos in those early years for the burgeoning Bomber Command, with squadrons gearing up for war and newer and larger aircraft coming into service. Hardly had they time to settle down in their new station, when on the 13th of January 1940 they were ordered to move again. Alan navigated his Wellington to Stradishall, an airfield in Cambridgeshire. Almost immediately training began and Alan manned the unique under gun turret, a new concept for the Wellington. Pre-war bombers such as the Heyford had been fitted with an under turret called the 'dustbin' and later the Whitley had this form of defence. It was called the dustbin as it could be lowered and raised and had the same shape as that type of receptacle. However it was discovered that the under turret was of little value for defence, as almost all fighter attacks came from the rear port and starboard quarters. One feature of the later British bombers such as the Lancaster, Halifax and Stirling was the almost total lack of under turrets, yet by late 1943 the Luftwaffe had perfected what was known as 'Schrage Musik. (which translates into-Jazz Music or Slanted Music) Schrage Musik was upward firing cannon carried by a night fighter; usually a twin engined Messchersmitt Me 410. This powerfully armed aircraft was to wreak havoc with the massed bomber streams by manoeuvring under the bomber and raking it with cannon shells. Almost all types of American bombers carried a 'Belly Gunner' or Ball Gunner as the luckless crewman was called.

Alan continued his training sorties with the squadron, but on the 8th of March he completed that training and was posted to No 99 Wellington Squadron at Newmarket. After settling in with his squadron and getting to know the run of things and his fellow aircrews it was a case of just waiting. It was with this squadron that Alan for some obscure reason was given the nickname of 'Bill'. It has never been discovered exactly why he was given this name, but it might be assumed that it was a slight play on the words of the name 'Bill Bailey' from the famous song. Whatever the reason, he was Bill Broadley to all those with whom he served. (For reasons of clarity and formality Alan will be the name used forthwith)

Alan's school friend and cousin Jimmy Wray volunteered for the RAF some six months after Alan, and like him, he volunteered for aircrew. He was told to report to RAF Cardington in Bedfordshire for categorisation.

He duly arrived, was given all the usual tests and a medical and then promptly sent back home to await a further call. During his interview it was discovered that Jimmy was technically qualified in radio. He had always dabbled in building his own radios when at school and the 'Brass' at Cardington noted this. A couple of months after returning home he received a letter asking him to report to Swanage in Dorset. Swanage turned out to be a Government secret radar establishment. Jimmy Wray was to spend the entire war in radar research and development flying in a great variety of aircraft. For Alan being part of No 99 Squadron meant the training sorties for qualification was complete and from this point on, flying was to be for real. With all the apprehension of a 'Green' bomber crewmember he waited. The waiting was not for long, on the 17th of March 1940 he carried out his first operational sortie. Dalesman, Alan Broadley was going …

Chapter Three

To War

With Flight Sergeant Snowden as his pilot and Pilot Officer Holford as the 2nd pilot (called the 2nd Dickie in RAF jargon) they took off in Wellington N 2914 at 1010hrs on a sweep of the North Sea in search of German naval units. After a fruitless search lasting 4hrs 20mins they landed back at Newmarket feeling rather deflated. Searching the sea for a ship was both tiring and dispiriting, but for Alan it was a valuable first lesson in operational flying.

MARCH.					Time carried forward:—	112·25	
Date	Hour	Aircraft Type and No.	Pilot	Duty	Remarks (including results of bombing, gunnery, exercises, etc.)	Flying Times Day	Night
17/3/40	10·10	WELLINGTON N.2914	F/S SNOWDEN P/O HOLFORD	NAVIGATOR	SWEEP FOR GERMAN NAVAL UNITS	4·20	

The entry in Alan's Flying logbook showing his first op.

In the early days of the war, the bombers operated by day, it wasn't until mid to late 1940 that the futility of flying and bombing by day over Germany was realised, but Alan was to fly one more 'daylight' before flying at night was to become the norm. However that 'sweep' was operational sortie number one for Sergeant Alan Broadley. A similar sortie was carried out on the 19th with similar results. From the 20th to the 29th of March it was training sorties almost every day with Alan acting as the Bomb Aimer in his role as the Observer. On the 31st Alan flew his first sortie over the German mainland. The sortie was what was known as a 'Nickel' raid. Nickel raids were in fact leaflet dropping sorties, showering the German population with notices telling them that the war was futile and that they should give up. The German city to receive this dubious load of propaganda was Hamburg with a reconnaissance of the River Elbe thrown in for good measure. This op was a night sortie and they took off at 2005hrs and landed safely at 0510hrs after a trip lasting 4hrs 45mins. Bomber crews resented putting their lives in danger simply to drop leaflets on the enemy, as they knew that it was pointless and of no value. In the sardonic language of the times, they called the aircraft that carried out those raids-'Bull shit bombers'

On the 12th of April they carried out daylight patrol of the North Sea and the attempted interception of the German battleship Scharnhorst plus other vessels off the Norwegian coast. This was the largest bombing raid so far in the war, and accordingly the losses were higher. Six Hampdens and three

Wellingtons were lost, all being shot down by fighters. Bombers carrying only two gun turrets one in the nose and one in the tail were particularly vulnerable to fighter attacks. The German fighters soon learnt to formate alongside or attack the Wellington from the side when neither turret could bring to bear any return fire. This problem led to a power-operated mid-upper turret being fitted into the four engined heavies that were to come into service later in the war. That raid on the 12th of was the last of the regular daylight raids of the war, from then it was night raids. Daylight raids on a regular basis were to begin again in the last year of the war. There were to be the occasional daylight raid, but as in the early days, the losses were unacceptable. On the 20th of April, Alan carried another bombing raid this time on the airfield at Stavangar in Norway. This raid was in support of the doomed campaign in Norway. They took off and attacked the airfield and headed for home. They were airborne for more than seven hours and due to low fuel reserves they had to divert Leuchars in Scotland. After each sortie crews had to attend an interrogation and make their reports to the intelligence officer, each crewmember relating his part in the raid and anything that was of special interest. As always, when they weren't on operational sorties, crews trained almost none stop. On the 27th of April Alan acted as navigator on a thirty minute engine test flight in a Wellington captained by a certain Flying Officer Percy Charles Pickard. This almost casual meeting between Alan Broadley and Charles Pickard was to be the start of one of the most famous flying partnerships of the entire war.

A Yorkshireman (from Sheffield) Charles Pickard was a pre-war RAF officer who showed great flare for flying and a tenacity to fight the war almost non-stop to very the end. Standing six feet four, with a shock of wavy blonde hair, and with an habitual briar pipe in his mouth, Pick, as he was affectionately known, literally stood out amongst his peers. He was just twenty four years old, but looked at least ten years older, which seemed to give him that extra air of authority. To add to this aura, his sister was married to the actor Sir Cedric Hardwicke. Pick was very rarely seen without his pet dog, Ming, a black and white Old English Sheepdog. Ming was to be his constant companion and travelled with him to each station whenever he was posted and she was even given her own flying Dog-Log-book. Ming was to learn when her Master was returning from an op and would whimper and pace up and down long before those around could hear engines of the returning aeroplanes. Alan Broadley and Charles Pickard, two very disparate men immediately struck up rapport and developed a very strong friendship, a friendship that was going to bring them together for many more operational sorties. Pick was married and already versed in operational flying and was a seasoned flyer. His navigator/observer, Alan Broadley, was the antithesis of those attributes. Quiet and reflective and a bachelor, albeit with Kitty forever in his thoughts. He was to be the calming influence for the mercurial Charles Pickard. On the 28th of April, with Alan acting as the navigator and Pick as the Captain they carried out a cross-country flight and oil consumption test. On the late evening of the 2nd of May 1940 Alan and Charles Pickard set off on the first of their many operational sorties. This op was patrol of German Seaplanes bases at Wangerooge and Borkum. It was a fairly straightforward even if a somewhat tiring op, they landed safely at Mildenhall in Suffolk after a trip of 5hrs 25mins. There is nothing in Alan's logbook to suggest that there were any problems on their return to make them divert to Mildenhall. However, the next day they flew a thirty minute air test which does suggest that they may have had engine problems.

It was at this time in May that the 'Phoney War' was to end and the German advance in Europe was to begin. On the 10th of May, German troops invaded Holland and Belgium with airborne landings at key points in those countries. The famous Maginot Line was breached with stunning success and with very few losses to the advancing Germans. The famous Blitzkrieg had begun. The BEF (British Expeditionary Force) had taken up prepared positions chiefly in Belgium with a small deployment in France as they had in 1914, but Holland was completely overwhelmed in a matter of days. This put enormous pressure on the BEF who after being hammered almost non stop, retreated steadily to the sea. Within days, the BEF was virtually cut off and so Bomber Command was ordered into action to support the beleaguered British Army. There were RAF Squadrons in France and Belgium, but the attrition rate was steadily eroding what reserves of aircraft there were. Outdated aircraft such as the Fairy Battle, Bolton Paul Defiant and the slow but graceful Lysander were being shot out of the sky with impunity. The Hurricanes of Fighter Command were putting up very strong resistance, but they too, were being overwhelmed. It was decided that Bomber Command should attack the airfields held by the Luftwaffe in Holland and the Low Countries.

On the day very that the Blitzkrieg began, Alan Broadley and Pick were in action attacking those very airfields. From the 10th to the 30th of May they flew ten operational bombing sorties in aid of the BEF. They attacked targets in, Namur, Liege, Charleroi, Mons, Valenciennes, Le Cateau and Conde, most of which had been famous battlegrounds of the Great War. The first raid was to airfields in southern Belgium, the last to Hazebrouck in northern France. These raids were the ongoing attempts to stop the Luftwaffe from giving air support to their advancing armies and prevent the overrunning the BEF whose position was becoming increasingly desperate as the retreat to Dunkirk got underway. Fighter attacks on the bombers were constant and ferocious but the Flak counted for most of the losses and many bombers were shot down. Luck was with Alan and Pick and they fought their way through what appeared to be a one sided battle. Grievous damage was being done to the advancing German columns but scores of RAF aircraft and crews were being lost, some being taken prisoner, but the majority being killed. On the operation to Charleroi-Namur, one of the Wellingtons from 99 Squadron was shot down by Flak. The crew of Wellington L7803 LN was; F/O Dyer DFC F/O Williams, Sgt Lawrenson, ACI Morton, and AC1 Ogilvie, LAC Lovejoy. The entire crew was killed and buried at Belval. It is interesting to note that even so long after the Air Ministry directive stating that all aircrews would hold the minimum rank of sergeant, there were still three members of that crew that were still aircraftmen.

Despite the efforts of the RAF, the soldiers on the ground in France were convinced that the RAF was not there. This is understandable as the nature of air warfare is such that attacks on enemy troop concentrations are carried out on the rear and advancing echelons and not over the actual battlefront. Alan explained this to Kitty and he was a little put out that the army thought the RAF weren't giving them full support. On the 30th of May the evacuation of the BEF from Dunkirk began when the defiant BEF finally went into retreat. Despite determined German air attacks, the ships of the Royal Navy assisted by scores of small ship and pleasure boats set about picking up many thousands of troops. By the time of the sortie to Hazbrouck on the 31st of May, 'Pick' Pickard had been promoted to Flight Lieutenant, one of many promotions to come. On each of those bombing sorties, Alan had acted as navigator, the crew position that he was going to occupy permanently, with the bomb aimer cum gunner roles to be left to the specialists. It was after this series of sorties that Pick recognised that he had in the newly promoted Flight Sergeant Broadley, a navigator of extraordinary ability. In June, 99 Squadron was well and truly in the thick of the air battle raging around Dunkirk and the advancing German armies, and by the 4th of June, the 'Miracle of Dunkirk' had been accomplished. Under the very noses of the Wehrmacht and Luftwaffe, more than a third of a million troops had been rescued from the beaches of Dunkirk. Although bereft of armour and artillery, the nucleus of an army was intact. On the final day of the Dunkirk evacuation, Bomber Command was back to attacking targets in the German heartland but still striking at the German forces in Northern France and Belgium. Alan and Pick were on one such raid to Germany when they bombed Dusseldorf and Mannheim. On the 10th of

June, Italy declared war on Great Britain bringing a number of fresh targets for Bomber Command to attack, stretching still further the resources of the RAF. On the 15th of June, Alan and his crew were briefed for a somewhat long sortie that entailed flying to two bases in England and to four bases in France. They took off from Newmarket at 0730hrs, landed at Northampton, flew to Poole in Dorset, refuelled and headed to St. Cast-Nantes, then onto Bordeaux then Toulouse finally landing at Salon in the South of France. At Salon the RAF had a small detachment of bombers from where they were to attack targets on the Italian mainland. From Salon, Alan and Pick flew across the Alps with seven other Wellingtons to the Italian city of Genoa. The attack was a complete failure as only one Wellington actually bombed the target. They returned to Salon and on the 16th they took off once more with twenty one other Wellingtons to attack Genoa, Milan and Bresso. This raid was a success inasmuch that all bombers attacked the targets and all returned safely. They returned via the French and English airfields and landed safely at Newmarket after an aggregate of some twenty three and half hours of flying. There was no time for rest, save for a twenty four hour recuperation and then it was back to operations. Despite the hectic schedule of bombing operations, Alan managed to write to Kitty at least once a week and she to him. Kitty was well aware of the danger that he faced, but like thousands of other sweethearts mothers and wives she kept her feelings and fears to herself. To keep those fears at bay, she set about concentrating all of her energies into her studies. Though still only eighteen years old, it wasn't to be long before she would be moving on to a teachers training school to train as a physical education teacher. Alan took leave as often as he was allowed, but with the war situation as it was, flying came first. Kitty remembers fondly how Alan brought French perfume and silk stockings from the time when he was detached to Salon.

On the 19th of June they were briefed for an attack on the city of Essen in the Ruhr valley, the heart of the German industrial zone. The Ruhr was the most heavily defended area in Germany and was to become the graveyard of Bomber Command. In mid 1940 the Germans had not perfected the Flak/searchlight/fighter defence system which were to decimate Bomber Command some two years later, but nevertheless, the defences that the Wellingtons of 99 Squadron and others had to face were still very formidable. It must be remembered that the navigation aids available to the command in 1940 were very primitive and the European weather was as much an enemy as were the Germans. There were 112 aircraft on this raid. 53 Hampdens, 37 Wellingtons and 22 Whitleys. The targets were the storage depots and railway junctions between Hamburg and Mannheim. Pick as the

Skipper, Pilot Officer Thomas as the co-pilot, Alan as navigator, and Sergeants Mills, Hanigan and Harniman they took off in Wellington R-3200 O-Orange at 2235hrs and headed for the target at Essen. On reaching the target area the Flak was thick and heavy but all the bombers fought their way through. Over the target Sgt Mills dropped the bombs and Pick turned the Wellington for home. As they were leaving the target area, a burst of Flak hit the starboard engine causing it to seize up almost immediately. Wellington O -Orange was in trouble. Pick and P/O Thomas headed the bomber west making for the relative safety of the North Sea. It was a struggle to maintain height, and due to the great strain placed upon the port engine, the oil pressure was dropping at an alarming rate. Nursing the aircraft, Pick fought to maintain altitude, but he knew he was fighting a losing battle. The white wave tops of the North Sea loomed ahead of them and the Wellington sank ever lower. The wireless operator sent an SOS to Newmarket and then they prepared for the worst. Realising that they would have to ditch, Pick gave orders to the crew to man 'Ditching Stations' Cutting the labouring port engine he held the aircraft off as long as possible keeping the nose up.

O-Orange bellied into the water and stopped almost immediately. Although the crew was strapped in and ready for the impact, none expected such a dramatic rate of deceleration. Pick's huge six feet four inch frame was smashed against the instrument panel, breaking his watch and damaging his wrist. Surprisingly no other member of the crew was hurt. Although the dinghy was self inflating, the crew had taken no chances and inflated it as soon as they began the evacuation. They all scrambled aboard save for the rear gunner who had become entangled with a radio aerial which had wrapped itself around his neck. Alan Broadley swam to his aid and cut the offending wire with the knife he always carried with him and dragged the gunner aboard. Once in the dinghy they prepared for a spell in hostile seas and a hoped for rescue. Once they had all more or less settled in, they decided to divest themselves of all the heavy clothing they were wearing, especially the rear gunner who was swathed in three layers of clothing. They watched Wellington O-Orange settle deeper in the water and then slide gently beneath the waves. Although the sea was not running high, the waves were choppy enough for the water to slop over the sides of the dinghy causing cold and discomfort to the crew. Not only did it cause discomfort; it weighed heavily in the dinghy. Pick had by far the largest feet and therefore the largest flying boots so his were used to act as a bailer to empty the water back into the sea. Aircrews of Bomber Command were always issued with escape aids to help them to escape and evade if ever shot down over enemy territory. Pick unscrewed the top of a button from his tunic where the base of the button revealed a miniature compass. Handing it to Alan, he is reputed to have said, "Right Bill, You have heard of the Ancient Mariner? Well you are now the Instant Navigator" This is probably apocryphal, but this is the sort of quip for which Pick was renown. However, humorous remarks or no, nothing could hide the fact that they were in a desperate situation. Under the direction of Alan, the crew took turns to paddle the best they could in the general direction of the English coast. They were hopeful that a search had been organised for them and this kept up their spirits. As they made painfully slow progress to England, a hole appeared in the bottom of the dinghy, which was promptly plugged by the foot of one of the crew. After a few more hours of paddling, one of the crew became somewhat depressed and miserable and started to complain. This had the effect of upsetting the rest of the crew. Pick never could and did not countenance such behaviour and took the crewman to task reminding him of his duty, which seemed to have the desired effect.

Back in England a search had been launched and several hours after being reported missing, a search aircraft from their squadron was despatched. When they heard the aircraft engines, Pick fired off a Very light. This had a dramatic effect, and they were spotted. That was the good news, the bad news was that they were floating right in the middle of a minefield. The search aircraft dropped supplies but that is all they were able to do other than orbit the dinghy until the dinghy cleared the minefield. Eventually it was considered safe and a rescue launch from the Air Sea Rescue Service Cox'nd by Flight Sergeant Len Ambler (later Flt/Lt Ambler MBE) was despatched to the general area.

16/6/40		WELLINGTON P. 9275	F/LT PICKARD P/O THOMAS	NAVIGATOR.	SALON - GENOA - MILAN - [illegible] - RETURN		5·10
17/6/40	10 30	WELLINGTON P. 9275	F/LT PICKARD P/O THOMAS	NAVIGATOR	SALON - CASTRE - BORDEAUX - NANTES - ST. CAST - POOLE - NORTHAMPTON - BASE	6·55	
19/6/40	22·35	WELLINGTON R. 3200	F/LT PICARD P/O THOMAS	NAVIGATOR	BASE - ESSEN - CRASHED IN N. SEA [illegible] ON RETURN. PICKED UP AFTER 14½ HRS.		4·45
					TOTAL TIME	172·00	106·25

The entry in Alan's Log-book reporting the crash in the North Sea.

When O-Orange crashed into the sea throwing Pick against the instrument panel, his watch had stopped at 3-20am the time of impact. At something like 5-40pm, fourteen and half-hours later, the sodden and tired airmen of Wellington R-3200 were hauled aboard that rescue launch. There were two aircraft lost on that raid of the 19th, one Whitley and one Wellington, Pick's O-Orange.

14 HOURS ADRIFT IN DINGHY

R.A.F. MEN'S PLIGHT AFTER RAID OVER GERMANY

Pilots of their own squadron helped to save the crew of a British bomber which was forced to come down in the North Sea while returning from a raid over Germany.

The crew of six drifted for nearly fourteen hours in a rubber dinghy before they were picked up.

In the early hours, while over the sea, engine trouble developed. The pilot immediately sent a message to his base and soon after the aircraft began to lose height fast.

S O S SENT OUT

At 3,000 feet an S O S was sent out, states the Air Ministry news service. Though the pilot brought the aircraft on to the water as well as he could, it struck a wave and plunging into the sea nose first remained submerged for a few seconds.

When it came to the surface the tail was well in the air and the fuselage above water. In the four and a half minutes before the aircraft sank all members of the crew escaped. While the rear gunner was climbing out the wireless aerial got caught up round his neck. The observer cut the wire with his knife.

When safely in the dinghy the crew threw away their heavy clothing. They kept a pair of shoes to bale out the water which at first half filled the dinghy. Later they used the shoes to paddle the dinghy and navigated by the captain's compass. A small tear in the bottom was effectively plugged by the foot of one of the crew.

LOCATED BY BOMBERS

At the squadron's base in England pilots were volunteering to take part in the general search, and eventually one of them, guided by a Verey cartridge fired from the dinghy, located the crew. Having wirelessed the position the bomber circled the area for nearly three hours, keeping the dinghy in sight all the time.

Later it was relieved by another aircraft from the squadron which remained over the dinghy until the six men were picked up by the launch which had been sent out.

R.A.F. BOMBER CREW SAVED FROM SEA

PADDLED RUBBER BOAT WITH SHOES

Pilots of the same squadron helped to save the crew of a British bomber which came down in the North Sea while returning from a raid over Germany.

The crew of six drifted for nearly 14 hours in a rubber dinghy before they were picked up.

Engine trouble developed while the 'plane was over the sea. The pilot sent a message to his base.

Soon the aircraft began to lose height fast. At 3,000 feet an S O S was sent out, says the Air Ministry News Service.

A Nose Dive

Though the pilot brought the aircraft on to the water as well as he could, it struck a wave and, plunging into the sea nose first, remained submerged for a few seconds.

When it came to the surface the tail was well in the air and the fuselage above water. In the 4½ minutes before the aircraft sank all members of the crew escaped. While the rear gunner was climbing out the wireless aerial caught round his neck. The observer cut the wire with his knife.

When safely in the dinghy the crew took off their heavy clothing. They kept a pair of shoes to bale out the water, which at first half filled the dinghy. Later they used the shoes to paddle the dinghy, and they steered by the captain's compass.

A small hole in the bottom of the dinghy was plugged by the foot of one of the crew.

Search Volunteers

At the squadron's base in England pilots were volunteering to take part in a search, and eventually one of them, guided by a Verey light fired from the dinghy, found it.

Having wirelessed the position the bomber circled the area for nearly three hours. Later it was relieved by another aircraft from the squadron, which circled over the dinghy until the six men were picked up by a launch that had been sent out.

As a result of their ordeal the whole crew was put into hospital for a couple of days and taken off operations for the next ten days. Alan wasted no time in heading straight for Leyburn and to Kitty. Alan related his ordeal to her but he didn't dwell on it. He confided in her that the idea of death didn't trouble him as such, but death by fire was his great worry. All too soon the ten days leave came to an end and it was back to 'work. '

A six hour trip to the Black Forest area of Germany on the 29th of June was followed by four more trips to Bremen, Wilhelmshaven, back to Bremen and then the Ruhr all within the first three weeks of July. Alan's log book shows that he did not fly in the month of August. This was due to a short detachment to RAF East Wrethem in Norfolk, the home of No 311 (Czech) Squadron. After the sortie to the Ruhr in July, Flt/Lt 'Pick 'Pickard was promoted to Squadron Leader and posted to command and train 311Squadron. On completion of his flying tour of operations, not only was Pick promoted, he was also awarded the Distinguished Flying Cross (DFC) the citation appearing in the London Gazette on the 30th of July 1940. After arriving at East Wretham, he wangled it that Flt/Sgt Broadley be detached to help with the ground navigation planning. This was approved, but by the middle of September, Alan was back with 99 Squadron, so it appears that it wasn't really official. Alan carried out one more bombing mission with 99 Squadron, his twenty eighth and then he was taken off operations for a rest. In the jargon of the RAF he was 'screened' from operational duties.

Being screened did not mean he was screened from flying, for within a week he found himself at No 20 O.T.U. (Operational Training Unit) Lossiemouth on the Moray Firth Scotland. Flying with an O.T.U was at times more dangerous than operational flying, for trying to teach 'Green' crews could be quite hazardous. By the 22nd of September he was acting as a flying instructor (Navigation) in an Avro Anson trainer aircraft ranging over the Scottish Highlands. That was the first of twenty one navigation and bomb aimer training flights he was to carry out at RAF Lossiemouth. He managed to get fourteen days leave for the Christmas, but by the 28th he was back in the air on a training flight. Then for the first time since he began flying, Alan was taken off flying completely and put behind a desk on ground training duties. For the months of January and February 1941 he taught the theory of navigation.

On the 1st of June 1941, Alan was posted to No IX Bomber Squadron based at Honington in Suffolk and returned to operational flying. His flight Commander on the squadron was none other than Squadron Leader Charles Pickard. The team was back together. At the beginning of the year Pick had been awarded the Distinguished Service Order (DSO) appearing in the

London Gazette on the 7th of March 1941. It was at this time that Charles Pickard became a film star, albeit for one brief film. The film was the famous 'Target for Tonight ' a wartime propaganda film. The British Government was deeply conscious of the feelings of the public and realised that the man in the street wanted to know if 'our boys' were handing out to the Germans what was being handed out to Britain. The Government in 1940 planned to make a film depicting Bomber Command hitting back and dishing out to Germany what the Luftwaffe had given to London, Coventry and half a dozen other cities in the UK. In the early spring of 1941 Pick was selected to 'Star' in the film as Squadron Leader Dixon, this meant he had to take time off from actual bombing raids with IX Squadron to shoot the film showing fake bombing raids. The film showed the crews in the briefing room, and preparing to take off into the night skies. The next sequences in the film shows Squadron Leader Dixon (Pick) flying over enemy territory dropping his bombs and wreaking havoc on German industry and returning with a severely damaged aircraft, but eventually landing safely. The 'Star' aircraft of the film was Wellington 'F' for Freddie. The film was a great success and achieved what it set out to do and that was to bolster public belief that their fearless young men were fighting the war to their utmost. Over the years the story has grown that Alan Broadley was the navigator in the film 'Target for Tonight' this is not so. The confusion came about due to Alan being Pick's regular navigator and it was assumed that he would accompany him. At the time the film was being shot, Alan Broadley was carrying out actual bombing raids with 99 Squadron. The irony was not lost on either of them.

On his arrival at IX Squadron, Alan learnt that he had been awarded the Distinguished Flying Medal (DFM) (London Gazette 23rd of September 1941 no citation) The DFM was in recognition of his unstinting skilful and effective navigating on more than thirty operational sorties and also for bravery under fire. This was nothing less than he deserved. Back in Richmond and Leyburn the award of the DFM to Alan had not gone unnoticed. Two local papers, The Northern Echo and The Darlington & Stockton Times both gave it full coverage. On hearing of his award, the Mayor of Richmond Mr. W. Robinson sent on behalf of all the townsfolk a congratulatory letter to Alan.

Borough of Richmond, Yorkshire.

Mayor's Parlour,
Town Hall
Richmond. Yorkshire.

?C/JK

29th September, 1941.

Dear Sergeant Broadley,

It was with great pleasure and deep pride that I learned that you, an old Richmond boy, have been awarded the D.F.M. for bravery whilst on active service with the Royal Air Force.

You are the first Richmond boy to receive this meritorious award and I send you my personal congratulations. As Mayor of the Borough, it is my privelege to convey to you, an expression of the congratulations and good wishes of Richmond folk here and everywhere; Richmond is proud of you.

Your father and I were boyhood friends, and so, to me, the announcement of the award is all the more gratifying.

Good luck and "Happy landings".

Yours sincerely,

W. Robinson

MAYOR.

Sergeant John A. Broadley, D.F.M.,
580819 Sergeant's Mess,
R.A.F. Station,
Newmarket.

The letter from the Mayor of Richmond on the award of the DFM

There was no time lost on celebrating. On the 9th of June they took off at 1620hrs-in daylight, for a raid on German shipping at Flushing and Calais. They attacked the shipping there but were themselves almost immediately attacked by no less than nine Messerhschmitt Me 109 Fighters. They fought their way out of the target area with both gunners giving a good account of them, and no doubt Pick's flying skills had kept them clear of further fighter attacks. They eventually landed safely at 2000hrs- in daylight. Alan's entry into his log book of this most dangerous of situations, is a nonchalant and laconic 'Attacked by 9 Me 109s'

Engine development was an ongoing process with the RAF and on the 16th of June, Pick and Alan flew a thirty minute air test in a new type of Wellington No W 5445 fitted with two of latest Rolls Royce Merlin engines, the very same engine that powered the Hurricane and the Spitfire. The Merlin was being continually modified and eventually was fitted to most of the later bombers in the RAF. The Wellington could carry a maximum load of 8,000lbs of bombs but the largest bombs weighed only 2,000lbs. On the night 16th of June, 99 Squadron Wellingtons lumbered off the runway and headed for Dusseldorf each carrying a 4,000lb bomb plus smaller ones, by far the largest and heaviest bomb ever carried by the RAF. Bomber Command was beginning to reply with ever greater bomb loads. After returning from Dusseldorf on the 19th they carried out one other raid and that was to Cologne and that concluded their operational flying for the month of June. In the month of July this seemingly inseparable pair flew seven more bombing missions, Essen, Cologne (twice) Munster, Bremen, Hamburg and Hanover. There was one further raid to Mannheim on the 5th of August, and then Alan was on the move once more. He was on his way back to Newmarket, but not to 99 Squadron but to 1419 Flight arriving there on the 6th and without Pick.

NO. 4. SQUADRON. HONINGTON.

Date	Hour	Aircraft Type and No.	Pilot	Duty	Remarks (including results of bombing, gunnery, exercises, etc.)	Flying Times Day	Flying Times Night
					Time carried forward:—	[illegible]	[illegible]
9/6/41	1620	WELLINGTON W. 5403	S/LR PICKARD	NAVIGATOR	BASE – FLUSHING – CALAIS – BASE (SHIPPING) ATTACKED BY 9. ME 109's	3.40	

The entry in Alan's logbook showing the attack by 9 Me 109's

Chapter Four

Paras & Clandestine Duties.

The value of Alan Broadley as a navigator had been recognised earlier in his service life and for this he had been awarded the DFM, but further recognition came when he was granted a commission and promoted to Pilot Officer. So as a commissioned officer, Alan settled into his new station and to a new type of operational flying. No 1419 Flight was a Clandestine Special Duties Flight operating modified Whitley bombers engaged in dropping supplies and agents of the Special Operations Executive (SOE) into enemy occupied territory. The SOE was not involved in espionage in the accepted sense; their role was to drop saboteurs and supplies to the Underground Movements in the occupied countries. Disruption of supplies, destroying troops trains and whenever possible, killing high ranking Germans was the principle aim of the SOE. For Alan this was an entirely different way to go to war and a new challenge. Navigation on Special Duties Flights had to be precise, there was no built in margin of error and only the best navigators were called to fulfil this role. Pilot Officer Broadley fitted the bill exactly. For the first three weeks with the 'Flight' Alan trained in the methods of operating with the SOE and all the dangers that he might possibly have to face when doing so. Special codes and navigation patterns had to be learned, and during those three weeks, he qualified as an Astro Navigator. All methods of escape and evasion had to be practised in the event of them being brought down in enemy territory. The consequences of what might happen to them if they were captured were spelled out in great detail. Working with the SOE meant danger but not necessarily from the flying side of the operations, but from what might happen if the were ever held by the Gestapo Although not an agent as such, this would not necessary save them from the horrors of incarceration in a Death Camp, torture and even death, so the same fate could await them that awaited the Agents. In short operating with Special Squadrons was dangerous in every sense. Once Alan had completed his ground training he had his first trip in a 1419 Flight Whitley and that was a one hour and fifteen minute run from Newmarket to Dishforth in Yorkshire, some 20 miles from Richmond.

In Richmond, Kitty Ovesby was making the final preparations to leave the Yorkshire Dales and take up her teacher-training course at the Chelsea College of Physical Education London. (In fact the Training College had been transferred to the village of Borth twelve miles from Aberystwyth in North Wales for the duration of the war) Alan had managed to get few days leave to see her before she departed, and no doubt, to visit all of his family and friends. All too soon he had to go back and after a fond farewell he departed for Dishforth while Kitty began to think about life in Wales and for a quiet country girl it seemed a very long way away from Yorkshire. On arriving at Aberystwyth she found that the entire course was to be accommodated in the Grand Hotel, which belied the Spartan conditions that the girls had to endure for the three years while they were there. All games instruction was done on the firm if sometimes wet sands, summer or winter. Gym work was done in the village hall except for one day per week when they were allowed to utilise the Girls School gym at Aberystwyth where they also used the local swimming pool. The practical teaching side of the training was done in the many local schools in the area, or if that was not possible, they practised teaching each other. The food was very basic at the hotel, consisting of, bread, soup, bread & cheese, bread & vegetable pie. Hunger was always a pervading feeling for the girls. They were remote from any sort of social amenities with just a single track rail link to Shrewsbury. To add to Kitty's feeling of isolation there was no half term holiday for them, so Easter, summer and Christmas holidays were looked forward to eagerly and were enjoyed to the utmost. The flow of letters between the two never stopped and this was a great comfort to a girl far from home.

Back at Newmarket Alan was nearing his first trip with the Special Squadron. After completing a container dropping test over Henlow on the 5th of August and a 30min air test on the 6th he was put on a briefing for Special Operations that very night. With Sergeant Reimer as his pilot they took off at 2015hrs and headed for Chateaureauroux France. On this S.D. Operation they dropped six 'Joeys' The name Joey was the code for an SOE agent. Although they carried these agents and dropped them over enemy territory, the crew very rarely got to know any of them, the higher ranking officers in the squadron who were involved in the planning would socialise with them. Often the first time that the crew ever saw these men and women, was when the entered the aeroplane. This was a deliberate policy, for if they did not know them they could tell anything about them. After dropping the Joey's, they headed for home and landed safely at Newmarket after an all round trip of 7hrs 30mins. Alan carried four further S.D. Operations with 1419 Flight to Copenhagen, Namur, Tours-Vierzon, Limoges-Toulouse with pilots Pilot Officer Hockey and Sergeant Reimer. The Limoges-Toulouse trip on the 6th of December lasting a weary 10hrs 30mins, was his last S.D. sortie.

On the 10th of December Alan, along with the now Flying Officer

Hockey was posted to No 51 Squadron based at RAF Dishforth in Yorkshire.The Officer Commanding 51 Squadron was none other than Wing Commander Pickard. The team was back together yet again. No 51 Squadron had recently moved from Linton on Ouse near York to Dishforth and as such was still in the early stages of working up to peak efficiency. Alan wasted no time in putting in for leave as he was close to Leyburn and Kitty who by this time had arrived home for the Christmas holiday would be waiting for him. He returned on the 22nd to conduct with Pick a search for a land mine that had supposed to have been dropped near the village of Thwaite in the Yorkshire Dales, not too far from Richmond. Could it be that Alan was flying his aeroplane over where Kitty lived? Nothing was found? On the 27th he and Pick took a 'Freshman' crew on a bombing raid to Boulogne. Freshmen crews were exactly that, freshmen or green crews carrying out their first operational sortie with Bomber Command. Freshmen were always given what was considered to be an 'Easy' op for the first one. Bomber crews very soon learnt that there was no such thing as an easy op, certainly not before it had been carried out! They arrived safely back at Dishforth after a trip lasting 5hrs 10mins. On the 29th it was a search in the North Sea for a dinghy that had been seen by an aircraft returning from a raid. Alan's logbook does not record if they found anything. They probably did not, as successful locations were usually entered. The month of January 1942 was very quite for the squadron but several obligatory basic training sorties were carried out. February by comparison was to be an exceedingly busy month. Alan and Pick had carried out just about every type of sortie that was possible with Bomber Command and SD Squadrons, and now with 51 Squadron at Dishforth, they were to be involved in a new concept of aerial warfare. On the 4th of February Alan and Pick began training the Whitley crews of the squadron in the art of dropping paratroops for a secret operation on the French town of Bruneval for what was known as 'Operation Biting'.

By 1942, the Germans had developed a chain of powerful radar stations along the coastline of France, Belgium and Holland. This radar, named Wurzburg, was so effective that it could detect British aircraft from a distance of some 250 miles and could quite easily pick up the massed bomber formations as they orbited for altitude before heading to the continent. The British Government scientists were very keen to get hold of the secrets of this radar. It was decided that a complete radar unit would have to be literally stolen, but how? A sea borne landing by the commandos was considered but discarded because speed into the area was critical. It was decided to drop the commandos by parachute and then take them off by sea, the commandos being defended by ground troops during the raid. So began the planning and training for Operation Biting. For Alan and Pick and the rest of the squadron detailed for the operation, it was low level map reading followed by more low level map reading. From the 5th to the 11th of February this is what they did. While Alan was carrying out all of this low level training, he celebrated if that's word, his 21st birthday on the 8th of February. On the 13th, Pick and Alan carried out a reconnaissance of the dropping zone near Le Havre, as photographic intelligence was vital to the whole operation. The photographs brought back by Alan and Pick were used by the Model Making Section at RAF Medmenham to build a scale model of the whole area surrounding the radar site. Flt/Lt Geoffrey Deeley, a former peacetime sculptor constructed and produced the model. The height of the cliffs, the fence barriers and the trees and shrubs were all painstakingly reproduced to scale to allow the troops taking part to study in detail all the problems that they may encounter. Major Frost (later of Arnhem fame) but currently with The Cameronians was selected to lead the ground forces for the raid on Bruneval. A Royal Air Force radar technician specialist, Flight Sergeant C.W.H. Cox was to accompany the paratroops and dismantle the parts of the apparatus that he was able, and photograph all that he could not. The rest was to be destroyed before the invading force left. Flt/Sgt Cox was to be accompanied by a section of the 1st Parachute Field Squadron of the Royal Engineers commanded by Captain Dennis Vernon. There was a rehearsal of the whole operation at Netheravon in Wiltshire on the 15th followed by a night training sortie dropping containers. The squadron then flew down to RAF Thruxton to prepare for what was to be the first British airborne commando raid of the war.

At 2215hrs on the 27th of February 1942 Whitley MkV Z9322 was the lead aircraft of twelve en route to the dropping zone at Bruneval.

The crew on that lead Whitley was;

W/Commander Pickard-Pilot
P/Officer Broadley-Navigator
P/Officer Porter Wireless Operator
P/Officer Judson Front Gunner/Bomb Aimer
P/Officer Hannant Rear Gunner

It is not the brief of this story to relate in detail all the events of the raid on Bruneval or Operation Biting, as it was officially known. Suffice to say that the operation went with precision and was a brilliant and stunning success. The radar components were safely dismantled and taken aboard a Royal Navy vessel along with the close up photographs of the components that could not be dismantled. The role of the RAF and in particular 51 Squadron was absolutely vital to the operation, but the greater part of the credit must go to the troops involved under Major Frost and to Flt/Sgt Cox the RAF technical expert on the operation. With the information obtained about the Wurtzburg radar, British boffins were able to produce electronic counter measures for the RAF aircraft operating over the continent. Shortly after the raid a newspaper carried the headlines. 'Led bombers on the Bruneval Raid' and went on to describe how Wing Commander Pickard led and commanded the aircraft on that daring raid and that he also piloted 'F for Freddie' in the film 'Target for Tonight'. The papers then described all the events of the operation at Bruneval and gave a résumé of the early life and RAF career of Pick. Very little was said about the actual seizing of the radar by the troops. For his part in leading the RAF squadron on the raid, Wing Commander Pickard was awarded a Bar to his DSO. Flight Sergeant Cox was awarded the Military Medal, a rare award for serving member of the RAF. Major Frost and Captain Vernon were each awarded the Military Cross for their excellent leadership and bravery during the operation.

27/2/42	1030	WHITLEY Z.9122	W/C. PICKARD	———	AIR TEST	·30	
27/2/42	2215	WHITLEY Z.9122	W/C. PICKARD	———	PARATROOP RAID BRUNEVAL		3·30

The entry in Alan's logbook for the Bruneval Raid.

The raid on Bruneval produced two minor tales of interest. Both were of tactical value with the second, involving Alan's cousin and school friend Jimmy Wray. As a result of the raid and the removal of vital components of the Wurtzburg radar, the Germans immediately surrounded all such sites with fencing, railings and barbed wire. The creation of these defences had the effect of preventing the local cattle from grazing in and around the sites. With no cattle to keep down the grass and weeds, the vegetation quite naturally grew longer and denser. On subsequent reconnaissance photographs, the long grass and weeds inside the compounds showed up very clearly along side the cropped grass on the outside thus making a perfectly identifiable target. The other result of the raid was that Jimmy Wray, who was working as a civilian technician on radar research at Swanage on the south coast, was moved along with the whole Radar Establishment further north. The relocation was undertaken to pre-empt any German version of the 'Bruneval Raid. So Alan's part in that raid, helped in a round about way, to have his friend Jimmy shifted from the south of England to the Midlands. Although geographically close to one another, to their disappointment they rarely managed to make their leave coincide, so their friendship though still strong was to be held in abeyance for the duration. The Bruneval raid was operational sortie number fifty two for Alan, but for the next three weeks he and Pick were taken off operations but Alan carried on flying doing Lorenz Beam flying tests with Sgt Cook and Flt/Lt Coates. The Lorenz Beam was a new type of approach beam landing system being tested by the RAF. The aircraft used on these trials was an old Miles Mentor, a twin engined training aircraft. On the 5th of March, Pick allowed Alan a full thirty minutes at the controls of the aircraft as they flew back from Newmarket back to Dishforth. This is marked very clearly in Alan's logbook, so it must have meant a great deal to him to be able to do some hands on flying. On the 6th it was a few days leave and Alan departed to his friends at Leyburn. All operational flying was carried out in the early hours of the morning, which really meant taking off in the late evening especially in the summer, carry out the raid and return in the small hours, the very time when the human spirit is at a very low ebb. Exhaustion was always a constant companion for Bomber Command crews.

His Majesty the King made many visits to his armed forces in the United Kingdom and on hearing of the deeds at Bruneval, it was decided that he should pay a visit to RAF Dishforth to speak to and meet the crews involved. He requested also that he might witness a practice drop by the paratroops that actually took part. Alan became involved in the practice exercise for the Royal occasion with training drops over Market Weighton and formation flying. On the 25th of March with everything organised down to the smallest detail the aircraft took off and prepared to drop with perfect timing over Dishforth, just as Their Majesties were to be entering the airfield as they had done at Bruneval. That was the plan. The Royal Party arrived at Dishforth on time, but, as was the wont of the King and the Queen, they stopped briefly to speak to the Guard of Honour parading at the station gates. As a result, by the time the Royal Cortege had appeared on the airfield, almost all of the aircraft had flown over and dropped their troops. In the end all that Their Majesties saw, was just two aircraft disgorging their sticks of paras. Alan who was in the lead aircraft with Flt/Lt Coates at the controls was well passed the airfield by the time the VIPs arrived. Pick with Major Frost were on the ground describing to the King and the Queen the sequence of events. The King who later dined at the Officers Mess, was gracious enough to accept that the slight hiccup in the proceedings was due to him. Royal visitors or not, the war had to go on for Pick and Alan. That very same evening they were briefed for a reconnaissance and Nickel trip to Paris. They took off at 1855hrs, carried out the photographing of the Paris locations, dropped the leaflets and returned safely at 0110hrs. As a result of their pioneering work with dropping those paratroops on the Bruneval raid and then the exercise before Their Majesties, Alan and Pick became the accepted experts in this new form of aerial warfare. From the beginning of April through to the beginning of July, Alan with a variety of pilots took part in several paratroop dropping exercises which included a company of newly arrived American airborne troops. On the 29th April, Alan had a special appointment. That appointment was to go to Buckingham Palace to have the DFM invested by H.M King George VI. Quite a nerve wracking experience for a diffident young man such as Alan.

In Whitley Z 9201 the next trip was to Genoa Italy-via RAF Wattisham in Suffolk for a photographic reconnaissance trip. This recce trip was the longest that Alan had ever undertaken and lasted an exhausting, 9hrs 10mins. On the May of that year, Pick was awarded a Bar (second) DSO, Gazetted on the 26th May. There was one break in this routine. On the 11th of July all para dropping exercises culminated in a grandstand exercise with a mass drop of troops and equipment before the Minister for Air, Sir Archibald Sinclair,

Air Chief Marshal Sir Charles Portal, Air Marshal Sholto Douglas and several generals. Not only was there a para dropping exercise but also there were two sections of Hawker Hurricane fighters, a section of Blenheims dropping smoke screens, 25 Whitleys dropping containers and further Whitleys towing Hotspur and Horsa Gliders. The exercise was spectacular success. That demonstration was the last exercise for Alan and Pick. On the 11th of that month they went home on leave ready for another posting. They flew to Dishforth and then to RAF Driffield in the East Riding of Yorkshire. Driffield was not to be their next station, but just a dropping off point for themselves and others who were going on leave in that part of the world.

In the summer of 1943 Brian Alderson now of Northallerton, was a fourteen year old trainee electrical motor mechanic at Jack Siddall's garage in Leyburn. One of the many jobs Brian was expected to do was to recharge wireless accumulators and car batteries then deliver them house to house. The going rate for the service was one penny for the charge and sixpence for delivery. When not out delivering, he served petrol and worked in the garage. He clearly remembers Alan Broadley pulling up in the forecourt of the garage in an Austin Ruby which had been loaned to him by his Uncle Jack. Brian will never forget the friendly smile and the way Alan wore his cap; at the regular jaunty angle. The car had developed a faulty wind screen wiper due to pin in the wiper motor working loose. Alan asked Brian if he had a 'young nail' meaning a very thin nail, which would replace the pin. Having the use of the car, meant that Alan could take Kitty out for a quiet country drive to visit his favourite part of Wensleydale, Pen Hill, a flat topped limestone outcrop that dominated the whole area, which could be seen for many miles. Once they got to the Dale, Alan would immediately relax and get his thoughts away from the war. With several days' leave to be taken, Alan made the most of it and relaxed with Kitty and his friends in Leyburn. He confided in Kitty that the Yorkshire Dales and Pen Hill in particular became a symbol for him when he was returning from bombing operations. They represented home. Kitty recalls of one time when Alan took leave and how he drove all the way from Yorkshire down to Wales to see her. Quite a journey for those days, with poor roads, a less than reliable car and strict petrol rationing. He arrived positively exhausted and simply slept for the first twenty four hours. Continuous flying whether on operations or training was very demanding and it was beginning to show. They spent a relaxing few days walking and talking and enjoying their precious freedom. Despite trying to forget the war, he spoke constantly of his fellow crewmen, but never of the war itself. Kitty likes to think that she got to know his crew through him although she never met any of them. Whenever Alan mentioned Charles Pickard, always spoke of him with great pride and admiration and said that he was lucky to fly with such an outstanding pilot. It was obvious that they both complimented one another. Pick the forthright forceful one, Alan the thoughtful but quietly determined one. Like all periods of leave,

Despite this, he spoke constantly of his fellow crewmen, but never of the war itself. Kitty likes to think that she met and got to know his crewmembers through Alan although she never did meet any of them. Whenever Alan mentioned Charles Pickard, he always spoke of him with great admiration and pride and said that he was lucky to fly with such an outstanding pilot. It was obvious that they both complimented one another. Pick the forthright forceful one, Alan the thoughtful but quietly determined one. Although Alan lived with his father and stepmother in Richmond, he never forgot his grandmother or his sister Anne of whom he was very fond and always paid them a visit at every opportunity the days passed all too quickly and Alan said his goodbyes and returned to his new air base which was No 10 Operational Training Unit at St. Eval in Cornwall. Kitty returned to her studies and tried to keep the constant worry of Alan and the war out of her mind.

Alan arrived at St. Eval on the 1st of August and embarked on a period of ground instruction. On the 18th he began flying from the base with a series of navigation exercises over the Atlantic Ocean. On The 27th of

August, St. Eval received an SOS from a crew of an aircraft that had ditched in the sea. A Hudson flying on a meteorological flight had belly landed in the sea. A Whitley had been despatched to search for the Hudson and that aircraft had also ditched due to both engines cutting out. Although both crews of each aircraft escaped the Whitley sank within seven minutes of ditching. Flt/Lt Osborne and Alan took off on an Air Sea rescue patrol to search for the missing crews. The Whitley in which Alan was flying located the stricken airmen who were all crowded into just one dinghy. A motor launch was sent out to their rescue and they were all brought back safely to dry land. Despite all this and his vital part in the locating of the dinghy, the entry in Alan's logbook simply states, 'Dinghy search - Dinghy found-crew saved' Although St. Eval was officially an O.T.U Alan and Pick were there not to train future crews, but for more clandestine operations. The Special Operations Flights being undertaken at St. Eval, was all part of the Special Operations being carried out by No 161 SD Squadron based at Tempsford in Cambridge. The Whitley aircraft had been detached to the base in Cornwall for a period of months in which Alan and Pick were to carry out several secret flights. The month of September was a busy one but apparently not for Special Duties. The secretive nature of the work carried out by these squadrons called for a high state of security and as such entries into log books by the crews were often very cryptic. For the month of September Alan and Pick carried out two Air Sea and Shipping patrols in Spanish waters each lasting 10hrs 45mins and 9hrs 30mins respectively, and one Special Fishery Patrol. The patrols in Spanish waters were daylight trips and the fishery patrol was a night operation. One can only speculate that they were on some clandestine duties at those times and the log book entries were just a cover. On the 23rd of September Alan and Pick carried out another sea search for a dinghy which had been sighted off the coast of Brest. As they were so close to German held territory they were given an escort of three Beaufighters. On return Alan entered the words 'No luck' in his logbook. Once more the sea had claimed a crew of a British bomber. In between these S.D. duties at St. Eval, Pick was carrying out S.D. duties in a Lysander at RAF Tempsford. The Lysander or 'Lizzie' as it was affectionately known to the crews, was a high wing monoplane, which normally carried a crew from one to three and was also used for Army co-operation flights. Alan never accompanied Pick on any Lysander operations as the pilot was the sole occupant and navigated this aircraft, the remainder of the space being taken up by equipment and/or agents. Occasionally two crewmen operated with them, but only under special circumstances. Pick however, allowed Alan several local flying trips in a Lysander and no doubt also let him fly the aircraft for a few minutes. On the 1st of October Pick was given the command of No 161 Squadron taking over from Wing Commander 'Mouse' Fielden. So Pick was in charge of operations.

On the 21st of October Alan was briefed for a Special Duty Operation. This S.D. trip was given the code name of Operation Monkey-Puzzle. The aircraft was the trusty Whitley and a crew of seven was carried. On a normal bombing operation only a crew of five was carried on the Whitley, on the SD ops there was an extra crewmember, to help with the dropping of all stores and agents. The crew for that night was

W/C Pickard-Pilot
P/O Prior-2nd Pilot
P/O Broadley-Navigator
P/O Taylor-W/Op
Flt/Lt Downer-Drop co-ordinator
Sgt Whitear-Rear Gunner.

The load they carried for that S.D. consisted of; two agents, four containers, and five packets. The containers were huge and filled the bomb bay of the Whitley. They took off at 2015hrs and headed for RAF Tangmere on the Sussex coast. There they refuelled, took off and climbed to 3,000ft and headed for Carbourg in France One feature of the S.D. Operations was the extreme low altitude that they were carried out. Bombers operated from anything from 16,000ft to 23,000ft so as to be clear of most of the Flak. The S.D. aircraft flew low to their target area before going even lower. The Whitely flew on to Blois and dropped to just a few hundred feet and waited for the signal light. The usual signal was given by the Resistance Workers was by an ordinary electric torch. Pick and his crew circled the town of Blois and saw a bright steady light and circled for fifteen minutes patiently waiting for the correct signal. After a short while longer a flashing letter 'L' could be seen from the ground. The usual response by the skipper of the aircraft was to 'burp' the engines of the aircraft intermittently. This Pick did several times, and after what seemed an age the final torch beam illuminated, indicating that it was indeed the Resistance men and not the Germans. They dropped the two agents and four containers from 500ft. They flew off to Marchenoir and dropped the five packages, crossed over the town of Gabour and headed for base. Six and half hours after take off; they landed safely at Tangmere. This rather brief and sterile account of a S.D. operation fails to bring over the sheer nerve wracking tension that was felt by all that were taking part. For Alan's part, his role as the navigator was made difficult from the start. Having to navigate onto a field in a foreign country and only torch lights to tell him that they were indeed over the field that had been selected for the drop, must have been an ordeal in itself. Despite all that, the entry in Alan's logbook reads, S.D. Operations as ordered, Loire- 6hrs 30mins. Special Duties were not restricted to the areas of France and the Low Countries as espionage was an ongoing activity throughout almost every country. On the 8th of November Alan was detailed to navigate a Whitely from his base to Gibraltar with P/O Cussens as his pilot. After a nine hour flight they landed safely at Gibraltar where they spent a pleasant ten days. His logbook does not state what they took out with them or whether it was a S.D. operation. In all probability it was and they would have taken took out a party of Agents. They were due to fly back to England and so on the 18th they carried out an air test on the Whitley. On the 19th they took off and set course to fly back to England. The air test the previous day must have been satisfactory, but on their way back while flying off the coast of Portugal they developed engine trouble and were compelled to divert to Hermaceo De Pera in Portugal. (A neutral country) The diversion turned into a crash-landing. They survived the crash without injury but were all interned by the Portuguese authorities. As always, due to the nature of Alan's work with the Special Squadrons and the SOE, the events leading up to and of being interned in Portugal are somewhat vague. At this juncture I must follow the information given to me by George Broadley Alan's younger brother. This information was passed onto George via his father and mother and is a reasonably accurate if sketchy account of the events.

When all of the crew had been taken into custody by the Portuguese, they were placed in confinement for a while until the British Embassy in Lisbon had been informed and the information relayed back to England. Each was allowed to send one telegram and one post card back to their families Apparently Alan was not in the least bit perturbed by his misfortune of being interned and seems quite cheerful and confident. After the flurry of telegrams and post cards, the task of actually getting out of Portugal became the number one priority. By now the whole crew were minor celebrities and were being feted by the local villagers with a party being organised in their honour. However the night before the party got underway, their flying boots were secretly stolen while they slept. This made them realise that there was something sinister going on and that they might be taken into permanent custody. Without much more thought or worry, they all set off 'shoeless' and walked the fourteen miles toward the Spanish border. Although it was in the middle of winter the temperature was quite pleasant and they very soon they were spirited out of Spain is unclear. No doubt the British Embassy like all Embassies had a well organised intelligence unit and escape lines. This unit would have got them out under noses of the German Legation in Madrid. All that is shown in the Public Record Office is a cryptic few words stating- 'Flying Officer Broadley and crew back at Temspford on Air Priority on the 19th of December 1942'

17/11/42	1100	Whitley [illegible]	F/O Cussen	—	Air Test	.30	
18/11/42	2246	Whitley [illegible]	F/O Cussen	Navigator	Gibraltar - Base. Crash landed Hermaceo de Pera (Portugal)		10.45

The entry in Alan's logbook when they crashed in Portugal.

It was January 1943 when Alan returned to Tempsford to resume his covert navigation role with 161 Squadron. On arriving at the station he discovered that the faithful old Whtitleys had been withdrawn and replaced by the Halifax Mk1. The Halifax Mk1 was a four engined bomber which, had been operating with Bomber Command for quite sometime, but was being withdrawn as the Mk11& 111 were coming into service. The Mk1 had shown that it was not suitable for night bombing operations because of its limitations in altitude, which resulted in heavy losses. However, as the aircraft used on the secret flights by the S.D. squadron rarely flew above 3,000 ft and often lower, it made them ideal for the task. The Halifax was a great deal larger than the Whitley, it was faster and had greater range, and of course, it had two extra engines. Over the following weeks, the crews of 161 Halifax Flight spent their time converting to their new charges. By comparison to the Whitley, Alan's 'office' in the Halifax was luxurious and a great deal warmer. So 1943 had arrived and with it a new aeroplane.

In mid January, Dorothy Pickard gave birth to a baby boy to be Christened Nicholas and to celebrate the occasion; Pick organised a party in the Officer's Mess. It was at this time that the well known impetuosity of Pick showed. As the beer flowed and all inhibitions vanished, Pick attempted to demonstrate his agility by hanging by his knees from a boxed in girder in the bar. It must have been a combination of his sheer size and the amount of beer he had consumed that caused him to fall. He fell very awkwardly on his right hand fracturing the thumb. He was carted off to the Station Sick Quarters and had the thumb and most of his hand encased in plaster. The injury didn't stop the intrepid Pick from flying. With one hand in plaster, he demonstrated to Squadron leader Hugh Verity how to land his Hudson at a much lower speed than the 'Guide Book' suggested, i.e. 75 knots, to a little above the stalling speed of 50 knots. Despite his plaster encased hand, and the injury, Pick demonstrated the technique by cutting the throttles of both engines as they passed over the boundary fence and

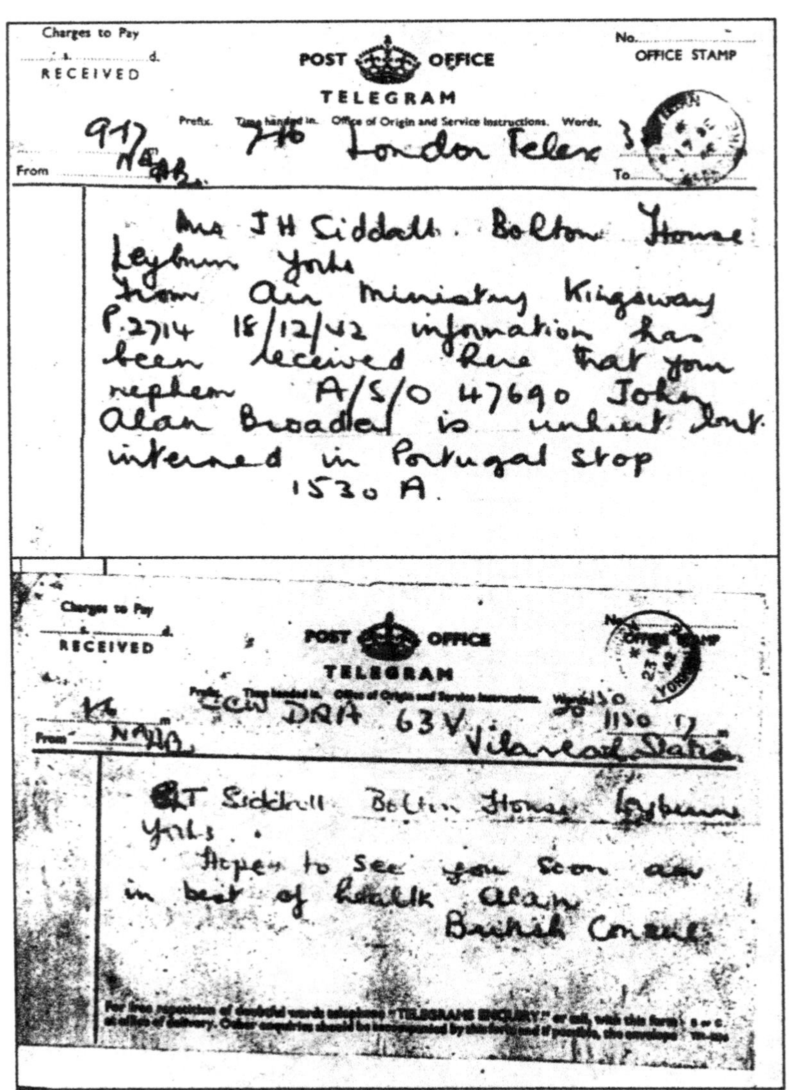
Charges to Pay
s. d.
RECEIVED
POST OFFICE
TELEGRAM
No.
OFFICE STAMP
Prefix. Time handed in. Office of Origin and Service Instructions. Words.
917 7.40 London Telex 3[illegible]
From NA[illegible] To

Mr J H Siddall. Bolton House
Leyburn Yorks
from Air Ministry Kingsway
P.2714 18/12/42 information has
been received here that your
nephew A/S/O 47690 John
Alan Broadley is unhurt but
interned in Portugal stop
1530 A.

Charges to Pay
s. d.
RECEIVED
POST OFFICE
TELEGRAM
No.
OFFICE STAMP
Prefix. Time handed in. Office of Origin and Service Instructions. Words.
K6 [illegible] DRA 63V 20 1150 [illegible]
Vilareal State
From NAHB.

[illegible]T Siddall Bolton House Leyburn
Yorks.
Hopes to see you soon am
in best of health Alan
British Consul

For free repetition of doubtful words telephone "TELEGRAMS ENQUIRY" or call, with this form, at office of delivery. Other enquiries should be accompanied by this form and if possible, the envelope.

Two telegrams from Portugal after Alan had been interned.

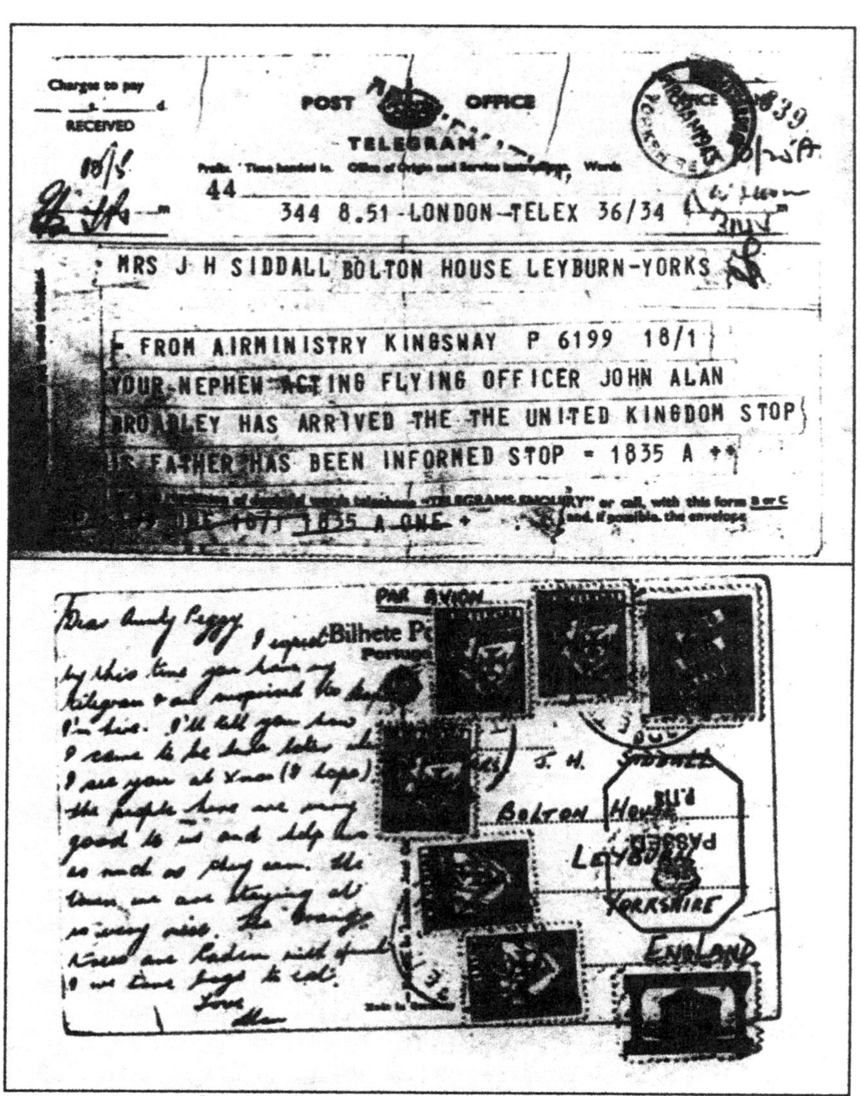

Charges to pay
RECEIVED

POST OFFICE
TELEGRAM

44
344 8.51-LONDON-TELEX 36/34

MRS J H SIDDALL BOLTON HOUSE LEYBURN-YORKS

FROM AIRMINISTRY KINGSWAY P 6199 18/1
YOUR NEPHEW ACTING FLYING OFFICER JOHN ALAN
BROADLEY HAS ARRIVED THE THE UNITED KINGDOM STOP
HIS FATHER HAS BEEN INFORMED STOP = 1835 A +

A telegram when Alan was back in the UK and a postcard to Aunt Peggy from Portugal.

applying the brakes as soon as the tail wheel touched the deck, achieving the short landing, the Hudson coming to a standstill in only 350 yards, a great improvement. Squadron leader Verity (Now Group Captain Hugh Verity DSO & Bar DFC) an experienced Lysander pilot was very impressed, and his earlier trepidation was allayed on the completion of the landing. This demonstration had a great bearing on the S.D. duties when landing in a field in France helping to achieve a faster turn round. The almost comical upshot to this story is that when the plaster was finally removed from Pick's hand, he went to the Mess to celebrate its removal and attempted to repeat the same party piece on the boxed girder. The result was the same as before, he fell and broke the same thumb, so once more it was encased in plaster. Broken thumb or not, it still did not stop him flying.
Within weeks of receiving the Halifaxes, the Flight was operational. On the 26th February with F/Lt Prior as his pilot, Alan carried out his first Halifax S.D. operation. This entailed a trip that lasted 5hr 30 min trip dropping several 'Joey's' and containers in the Loire area. All S.D. operations from Tempsford were actually carried out from RAF Tangmere the forward operating base. No. 161 Squadron also carried out photographic reconnaissance and Air Sea Rescue duties when they were not working with the SOE. The month of March was a busy time with photo/recce of gun sites on the coast of France, an ASR search, and S.D. operations in France when on one occasion they did not locate the target. The 'target' on S.D. runs was the code name for the Resistance workers. On the 13th of March Alan undertook his longest operational navigation run so far. They took off and were due to drop 'Joeys' and containers in Poland, a trip the Whitley could never have undertaken. When they were within twenty five miles of the target, the Halifax developed severe petrol problems compelling them to return to Tempsford. They had taken off at 1855hrs, and landed safely twelve weary hours later. It was a very long way to go to miss your target.
I would like to quote Mr. Tom Smith of York a former Flight Engineer with 161 Squadron at Temspford later in the war. He relates a rather poignant memory of when he was operating with 'Joey's. It was part of the engineer's duties to assist the 'Joeys' when they were about to jump, albeit just to open the drop out hatch. He recalls that almost always when a male 'Joey' was about to jump; he would raise his head and look beseechingly into the eyes of all those around-then drop out. The females 'Joeys' would calmly prepare, steady themselves and then go. No looking up, no eye contact. Tom Smith has never forgotten the apparent but quiet bravery of the women. He also says that on occasion, some 'Joey's funked the jump by pulling the 'D' ring allowing the 'chute' to spill inside the aircraft, thus nullifying the drop,

although this never happened on any of his S.D. drops.On the 24th of March, Pick was awarded a second bar to the DSO and this was recorded in the London Gazette 26th of March 1943. It is worth recording Pick's third DSO.
Wing Commander Percy Charles Pickard DSO & Bar DFC. This officer has completed a very large number of operational missions and achieved much success. By his outstanding leadership, exceptional ability and fine fighting qualities, he has contributed in large measure to the high standard of morale of the squadron he commands.
The brevity of the citation was due to the secret nature of the work that he was doing. For his service with No 311 Squadron, Pick had also been awarded the Czech Military Cross by the Free Czechoslovakian Government
With the arrival of April, Alan became involved in a different type of Special Duties and a new type of aircraft. The new aircraft for him was the Lockheed Hudson. The Hudson was a twin engined aeroplane of American manufacture but quite roomy and had a reasonable turn of speed, a fairly long range but most importantly of all, it could land in a very short distance so dramatically demonstrated by Pick some weeks earlier. Prior to the Hudson operations, he had been carrying out extensive 'GEE' training on twin engined Oxfords. The term 'Gee' was the name given to latest navigation aid which, was being introduced into Bomber Command. It was considered that the S.D. squadrons who navigated to within yards of their target would need this new aid also. So, Alan began his training for its use in the field of Special Duties, for him a new concept in navigation and S.D. work. On the 13th of April, Alan flew a Halifax operation to the Toulouse area dropping agents and container. His pilot on that trip was Squadron Leader later Wing Commander Lewis. (Now Air Chief Marshal Sir Lewis Hodges. KCB CBE DSO & Bar DFC & Bar) This was the first of several S.D. trips that Alan was to do with this distinguished officer. However it was with Pick that Alan was to carry out his first Hudson operation. On the 15th of April in his logbook, Alan referred to the operation as a 'Pick-up' but the entry is scrubbed out, as it was never their policy to enter what they were actually doing. It was a reasonable mistake as it was his first 'Pick-up' op; all previous work had been dropping agents and containers by parachute. A pick-up was when they rendezvoused with a 'Target' in France, the target being a group of Resistance workers. A pre-arranged field had been selected for the Hudson to land, do the drop and the pick-up turn round and take off. Apart from the fact they actually landed the aircraft on these ops, there was one other essential difference. All pick-ups were carried out in bright moonlight. Moonlight was absolutely vital, as they needed light to see the field and to land. The Hudson sorties from the navigator's point of view were

the most difficult. He was required to navigate within a few degrees, to a field selected some where in France, a field they trusted was reasonably flat and not deep in mud. The field also had to have no obstruction within the landing parameters. On finding the field, the crew would then look out for a series of signals given by the reception committee (French Resistance) who used ordinary torches in the form of an inverted 'L' to direct the aircraft in to land. A first time landing was always the best, but on many occasions it was a case of overshooting and going round again, giving the German forces all the more time to locate the area. On the 'Drop' code named Operation Dogfish, Pick along with Alan, had Flying Officer Cocker as his W/Op/Air Gunner. They took off and flew to Pont-de-Vaux and located a huge meadow code named 'Junot' close to the road to Arbigny. Their outward bound passengers were agents Francis Closon and Fraval plus 12 suitcases. Agents Bruno Larat and Paul Riviere were to be their reception committee When they taxied to a standstill and began the 'drop, they found they had a problem. They were expecting four passengers to be picked up, P. Lanque, H. Deschamps, G.Boisson, Martin, Fassiaux, and Dr. Robert Blochet, but there were eleven people waiting with a look of hope on their faces. Pick had brought along for the 'ride', Wing Commander Brooks and Wing Commander Lockart. The maximum number of passengers allowed was ten and so only eight of the hopefuls were to be allowed to board. This took several minutes to sort out and they were on the ground for more than fifteen minutes, much longer than any pick up should have taken. Eventually they took off and landed safely at Tangmere. On occasions, the field was less than adequate certainly for Hudson Pick-ups. Mud was always a problem and on one trip, Pick's Hudson became bogged down for what seemed an age as they and the French reception committee strove to dig out the recalcitrant aircraft. Someone neatly observed that Pick and Alan would go on Drops and Pick-ups armed to the teeth with revolvers and a whole variety of escape equipment, but not so much as spoon with which to dig out a sunken wheel of an aeroplane. This was the nature of Pick. He averred that if he were ever shot down and uninjured, he would somehow find his way back to England. There is little doubt that is what he would have achieved this given a half chance.

After that Hudson op, Alan received notice that he had been awarded the Distinguished Flying Cross (DFC). There is no doubt that Pick had a hand in the recommendation for the award of the DFC for Alan, as he more than anyone, knew how well and efficiently he had performed over the past two years of almost non-stop flying. The award was dated in the London Gazette on the 20th April 1943 and unlike the award of the Distinguished Flying

Leyburn County Council School 1925.
Alan is forth left from row. Jimmy Wray is third right front row and Anne is second left middle row.
Note the pocket watches worn by Alan and Jimmy.

Alan and Anne when under the care of Nurse MacDonald

George Broadley with his father and sister Anne.

**Sylvia Coates with;
Anne, Jimmy and Alan.**

The 'Marksman'

Richmond GS pupils. 1938
Alan is third left second row from the front

In the Lab.
John Gaine-Peter Squires-Barry Jones-Jeffrey Ottley-
Howard Nicholson-George Kinshin-Alan Broadley-Dennis Bell

Richmond G.S. Cricket First XI 1937

D.H.Atkinson-P.J.Pendlebury-J.A.Broadley-R.H.White-J.S.E.Rob-RoyMcGregor
R.D.Bell-G.L.Woolass-F.H.Pedley-J.N.Evans-J.R.Calvert.
S.H.Walker (Capt) A.B.Harrison

Richmond G.S. Rugby First XV 1937-38

J.A.Broadley-J.W.King-J.W.Sidebottom-P.J.Pendelbury
J.R.Cubberly-J.G.Ressor-T.R.Shaw-G.W.Trott-J.N.Evans-F.H.Pedley-R.D.Bell
Rob-RoyMcGregor-J.H.Gaine.
J.M.King G.Glover P.C.Williams

No. 14. BOMBING LEADERS COURSE
STANDING:- SGTs. ELLIS. OBRIEN. HANWORTH. STEWARD. SQUAD. 1.
SITTING:- SGTs. WIMHURST. BROADLEY. P/Os. TAPP. DUGDALE. DUFFIN. CARTER. BLUNDELL. SQUAD. 2.

Alan with Uncle Jack Siddall.

With Aunt Peggy

Jack Siddall's shop in Leyburn.

Kitty and Alan.

Two of Kitty's favourite pictures of Alan.

Alan wearing the DFC & DFM ribbons.

Kitty Ovesby.

With two nurses during his spell in hospital after his return from Portugal.

Standing next to the nose of a 161 Special Duties Squadron at RAF Tempsford.

Pick.

Inspection of No 161 Squadron Tempsford April 1943 by the Minister for Air, Sir Archibald Sinclair.
Pick is with the Minister, Alan is the second on the right-centre.

The Memorial Plaque at Tempsford.

D.S.O. AND D.F.C. FOR RICHMOND AIRMAN

His Second Visit to Buckingham Palace

Navigated 'F for Freddie'

Alan 1943

Jimmy Wray 1944

Alan and Pick in front of Mosquito F-Freddie.

Alan in the Navigator's position in the Mosquito.

The results of the raid on Amiens prison from the French Newspaper Le Courier Picard.

French Partisans carrying the bodies of Pick and Alan shortly after the crash.

The original wooden crosses on the graves of Alan and Pick.

Dorothy Pickard with Norman Didwell at the 1994 Memorial Service at Amiens.

The War Memorial in Leyburn.

FLT/LT. J. A. BROADLEY.
D.S.O. D.F.C. D.F.M. R.A.F.

George Broadley.

Lilla Broadley.

No 99 Squadron reunion at Newmarket.
Anne, George and his wife.
Anne is wearing Alan's medals.

Alan's medals.
Top centre are the;
Distinguished Service Order (DSO)
Distinguished Flying Cross (DFC)
Distinguished Flying Medal (DFM)

PER ARDUA AD ASTRA

ALAN & PICK'S GRAVES AT ST. PIERRE NEAR AMIENS

Medal which did not have a citation. The citation read;

Acting Flight Lieutenant J.A. Broadley. DFM. No 161 Squadron. Flt/Lt Broadley has flown as navigator since April 1940. He has fulfilled the duties of Squadron Navigation Officer with great success in two operational squadrons. On one occasion the aircraft in which he was flying came down at sea and it was entirely owing to Flt/Lt Broadley that the crew was rescued. On two other occasions he has been involved in air accidents, but this officer continues to show unabated enthusiasm for operational duties

When the Mayor of Richmond heard of the award of the DFC to Alan, he immediately sent another letter of congratulations to him on behalf of all the people of Richmond. Quite naturally the local press made much of the story and duly reported it in their first editions. In recognition of their prowess and their achievements, the Air Ministry commissioned an artist to paint both Pick and Alan's portraits in oils. They had to travel to London for the sitting and the paintings were very highly acclaimed, but not by the two aviators.

Alan was not just a navigator; he was the Squadron navigator or Navigation Leader, to give him the proper title. The Navigation Leader was the one who organised and routed all operational sorties for the other navigators of the squadron. A very responsible job, but one that Alan was eminently well suited. Special Duties flying with 161 was becoming a mix of Halifax drops and Hudson/Lysander delivery and Pick-Up sorties. Alan was to do one more drop with Pick and that was on the 18th of April which was code named 'Operation Zinnia' The torch flarepath in France was laid out by Michel Thoraval who was working for the French Army Secret Service. They took out 200lbs of freight and after a lengthy twenty minutes on the ground, they took off with eight passengers; Petijean, Koenig and his son, Colonel Guenin, Callot, Brohan, Michelin and Champion. The S.D. operations continued and when there was no moonlight, the Halifax drops carried on. On the 20th April, Alan flew a 7hr 20min S.D. op with S/Ldr Bob Hodges to the Rodez area. On completion of that Hudson operation of the 18th, the Pick/Broadley partnership was broken up once again.

On the 1st of May, Pick was promoted to Group Captain and posted to command RAF Lissett a bomber station in Yorkshire. Squadron leader Hodges was promoted to wing commander and assumed command of 161 Squadron. From November 1942 to April 1943, 161 had carried out ten Hudson pick-up operations with SOE, with Pick flying on five of them. And Alan Broadley played a great part in all of this. Kitty recalls one of the many long conversations she had with Alan during the spring and summer of '43

Borough of Richmond, Yorkshire.

Mayor's Parlour,
Town Hall,
Richmond, Yorkshire.

R/B/K.

30th April, 1943.

Dear Flight Lieutenant Broadley,

The Mayoress and I send you our heartiest congratulations on the award to you of the Distinguished Flying Cross. It was my great pleasure to send you a congratulatory message when you were awarded the Distinguished Flying Medal for gallantry in action, and I can assure you that the news of this "double event" has delighted the Corporation and the townspeople of the ancient and historic Borough of Richmond.

Richmond is proud of the bravery of its sons in the present conflict, and we shall continue to watch your career with deep interest and concern. At all times we wish you "Happy Landings."

Yours very sincerely,

Wm Robinson

Mayor.

Flt/Lieut. J.A. Broadley,
Officers Mess,
R.A.F. Station,
Tempsford,
Nr. Bedford.

The letter from the Mayor Richmond on the award of the DFC

when Alan alluded to those Hudson S.D. operations with Pick and how on a couple of occasions he failed to find the landing ground, but Pick never doubted his ability. Some of the reasons for failing were due to not receiving the correct torch signals or heavy ground mist that prevented him seeing the field. Despite these problems, Pick, forever the one who had to achieve the maximum results, stood by his navigator. Kitty also remembers Alan speaking of a Frenchman on the squadron by the name of Phillipe Livery-Level who at the age of forty five managed to be accepted into the RAF and train as a navigator. After flying with No 52 Squadron Coastal Command he managed to be posted to 161 Squadron on S.D. duties. His Gallic charm and determination to fly made a great impression on Alan.
The months of May and June was a very quiet time for Alan and 161 Squadron with just a series of cross-country training sorties. This was due in part to the lack of 'moons' as the SD Squadrons almost always operated in moonlight to facilitate ease of locating and landing. There was one special training sortie, special to Alan and Kitty but maybe not to the RAF. On the 23rd of June Alan and Bob Hodges took off at 1155hrs and headed to Worcester and then flew directly over to Borth in North Wales where Kitty was at the Teacher Training College. The trip was a comforting gesture for both.

JUNE. 1943. Time carried forward:—

Date	Hour	Aircraft Type and No.	Pilot	Duty	Remarks (including results of bombing, gunnery, exercises, etc.)	Flying Times Day	Flying Times Night
13/6/43	1430	OXFORD MA-2	P/O FORBES	NAVIGATOR	BASE — SNEDBURGH — BASE	1·00	
23/6/43	1155	HUDSON N 7281	W/C. HODGES	— " —	BASE — WORCESTER — BORTH — BASE	2·15	

The entry in Alan's logbook for the trip to Borth.

The latter part of July saw the beginning of a very busy period for Halifax, Hudson and Lysander S.D. operations. For Alan it began with a 5hr 10min Halifax drop to Belgium with Bob Hodges. Alan was taken off operations for short time to allow him to attend the portrait sitting at the Air Ministry. Prior to this appointment he had been promoted to the rank of Flight Lieutenant. On the 22/23rd of July it was back to ops. Alan and Bob Hodges were briefed for operation Gamekeeper. The landing field was coded as 'Achille' south east of Soucelles. Their passengers to France were J. Agazarian, Cadet Adlein Marisall and their passengers out of France were Raoul Latimer, Jean Pierre Carrez and Joseph Pans. However most importantly their controlling agent in France was a certain Henri Dericourt. This agent was to cause a great deal of concern within the SOE and the squadrons on S.D. duties. During the time of Alan's involvement with him there was little suspicion and the pick-ups went on as normal. On the 27th and the 29th July Alan carried out two air sea rescue patrols over the North Sea when on the second of those patrols their Halifax met three Junkers Ju 88 fighters. Once again his logbook states that simple fact 'Met 3 Ju 88' and does not record if there were any combats with those fighters. On the 19/20th of August there was another Pick up with Dericourt involving Alan, and the Hudson crew that night was Wing Commander Bob Hodges, Flt.Lt. 'Lofty' Reed and Alan and the operation was Dyer. On the 23rd/24th Alan flew his last S.D. trip with the same crew on operation Trojan Horse when the receiving agent was Paul Reviere. They took out one passenger, Lois Franzini and picked up Maurice Graff, Francois Maurin, Professor Armand Khodja and Sergeant Patterson an escapee/evader RAF flyer. After a six hour trip they landed safely at Tangmere and then returned to Tempsford.

To return to Henri Dericourt.

Henri Dericourt was a pre-war civil airline pilot with many hours of flying experience who had served with the French Air Force in 1939/40 but went back to civil flying once France had been occupied. He always let it be known that his ambition was to own a farm, but he never did have the wherewithal for him to do so. Later in the war he contacted the British Secret Service and offered to work in the field of sabotage. After being screened for his loyalty he was accepted and joined 161 Squadron at Temspford under Wing Commander Pickard. Oddly enough there were doubts about his loyalty but he was still given the very sensitive job of Air controller in France, i.e. organising the landing fields and receiving agents. Not only was he under a little suspicion by the authorities but Ming, Pick's faithful dog would have nothing to do with the Frenchman and bridled at his approach. Nonetheless he was duly parachuted into France to begin his work. In later months it was established that Henri Dericourt was a possible double agent and working for SS Sturmbannfuhrer Hans Kieffer and SS Sturmfuhrer Karl Boemelburg at 84 Foch Avenue Paris. Henri Dericourt managed to extract a promise from his SS masters not to interfere with any of the Pick ups. This was agreed so long as he, Dericourt, allowed the Germans to copy any mail and receive the names of agents. This worked for a long while and Dericourt kept up the pretence. In a relatively innocent but portentous aside, Pick, after returning from a Hudson Pick Up commented, "I cannot understand how after attempting several landings on the 'target' area, the suspicions of the local Germans were not aroused" The answer lay in the duplicity of Dericourt. The head of SOE Colonel Buckmaster organised for Dericourt to be brought back to England under the pretence of being awarded a DSO. (It was partially true, as Buckmaster had mentioned the possibility of the award) Once in England Dericourt was told of the SOE's suspicions and he never returned to France until after the war. He was kept under restricted activity until mid 1944 and then he was allowed to fly with the RAF, but only on internal flights. After the war he was tried but acquitted by a French court. There was one rather interesting comment by one of 161 Squadron's Lysander S.D. pilots, Squadron Leader Hugh Verity who, despite having all the information on Dericourt, still considered him to be a personal friend. A warm and telling sentiment that in the midst of war, a personal friendship meant exactly that. So, added to the inherent dangers of Special Duties Operations, Alan had unwittingly operated with a double agent who might quite easily have had him and those who flew on the S.D. operations, arrested. A sobering thought for all. A fuller account of the 'Dericourt Affair' appears in Hugh Verity's excellent book 'We Landed By Moonlight' (Crecy Publishing)

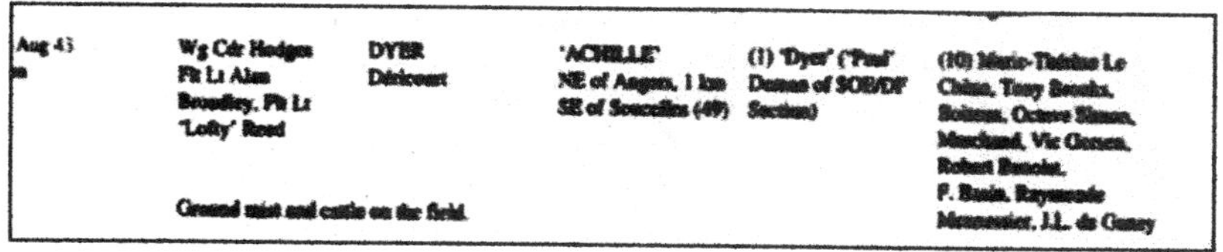

Aug 43	Wg Cdr Hodges Flt Lt Alan Broadley, Flt Lt 'Lofty' Reed Ground mist and cattle on the field.	DYER Déricourt	'ACHILLE' NE of Angers, 1 km SE of Soucelles (49)	(1) 'Dyer' ('Paul' Dumas of SOE/DF Section)	(10) Marie-Thérèse Le Chêne, Tony Brooks, Boiteux, Octave Simon, Marchand, Vic Gerson, Robert Benoist, F. Basin, Raymonde Mennessier, J.L. de Ganay

The 'Dericourt' S.D. drop taken from Hugh Verity's Book.

In September, the Pickard/Broadley team was brought together once more. From May 1944, Pick had been the Officer Commanding RAF Lissett and was thoroughly browned off with the tasks of the administration and general running of a bomber squadron. High ranking senior officer or not, Pick was determined to get back onto operations. After making many contacts and request to the Air Chiefs, he got his way and was appointed as the Commanding Officer of RAF station Sculthorpe, near Fakenham in Norfolk. Soon after taking up his appointment he arranged to have Alan posted to Sculthorpe as his navigator. The team was back together. Sculthorpe was part of 140 Wing of 2 Group, of the newly formed Tactical Air Force (TAF) No 2 Group's Air Officer Commanding (AOC) was the redoubtable Air Vice Marshal Basil Embry DSO & 2 bars, DFC & Bar, a man of vast experience. Early in the war Embry had been shot down and escaped by killing his guard and making his way back to England. He later commanded bomber and fighter squadrons and was a former Desert Air Force Leader. A formidable record. In Embry, Pick had met his equal, at least in character and personality if not in height. Embry was 5'6" as against the 6'4" of Pick. It wasn't too long before Pick and the rest were 'Basilised' by this forceful commander. On the 13th and 14th of September Pick and Alan carried out a one hour familiarisation flight in a Mosquito to Tangmere and back. The Mosquito was to be their new charge. This twin engined thoroughbred had more power; more speed and heavier bomb load than any comparable aircraft. It was arguably the best twin engined aircraft of the entire war. It was a fighter/bomber, reconnaissance and bomber and in April 1944 took on the role as the Berlin bomber from the Lancaster and Halifax. Unlike any other aircraft, the Mossie as it was known was made chiefly of wood and glue. This gave the aircraft great strength and great power to weight ratio, thus giving it, its speed and lifting capacity.

After those two short trips, Alan spent thirty two hours on an Airspeed Oxford fitted with 'Gee' navigation aid the navigation aid used with the Mosquito. He had operated Gee in the early days with the Halifax but with the new advances in radar technology he was required to retrain with the equipment. Alan and Pick were obviously training for more than the standard bombing raid. More training followed on the Mossie, with cross-country nav exercises, speed tests and bombing practise being the norm. On the 3rd of October the 'Team' was ready for their first action. Although flying in a Mosquito, it wasn't just any old Mosquito, it was F-Freddie, named after the faithful Wellington that starred with Pick in the film 'Target for Tonight' The target for F-Freddie and its crew was the power station at Pont Chateau and it was a 'daylight' raid, something the 'pair' had not done for some time. For this raid Alan was the Navigation Leader and he planned the route in and out for the squadrons that were taking part. No's 464 and 487 were the two squadrons involved, with No 21 being left on the ground as reserve, Alan had been actually posted to 21 Squadron but they both flew with 464 Squadron on the raid. AVM Basil Embry was to be in Command of the whole operation, and Pick was to be the leader of the first wave, with Embry flying in the last aircraft of the second echelon. There were twenty four Mosquitoes prepared for this raid, each carrying 4X500lb bombs each with an eleven second delay fuse. They took of at 1245hrs and flew to RAF Exeter to be bombed up and refuelled. They then took off again and flew low and fast across the English Channel straight to the target. They were met by very heavy Flak as they entered French airspace but their speed and altitude kept them out of danger. Pick's wave went into the power works at ultra low level, dropped their bombs and headed home. The second wave under the command of Embry, bombed from a shallow dive of 800ft. The target was completely flattened. As Pick banked F-Freddie away, a withering hail of Flak hit the starboard engine. He immediately switched off the fuel to the engine thus reducing the chance of a fire and powered on to the British coastline. With the engine now completely seized, he was unable to feather the engine (turn the propeller edges into the wind.) As a result this caused extra drag and slowed down their return. As a precaution they diverted to Predannock in Cornwall where they landed safely despite the damage. The return trip from Pont Chateau was 370 miles and the reliability of the Mossie had been tested to the full. Arriving at Predannock, Pick and Alan gave the engine a close inspection and decided that they could not wait for a spare engine to be sent, so they climbed back into the 'injured' F-Freddie and flew back to Sculthorpe on one engine, landing at 1730hrs. Five other Mosquitoes were hit by Flak on the raid, one having the navigator killed, the pilot; Wing Commander Wilson managed to bring the aircraft back to England. Although the target had been devastated, it was clear that the crews needed more low level bombing practise, and so that was the order of the day. Training and yet more training.

After that baptism of fire for Alan in the Mosquito, he received news of yet another award for bravery and leadership. He had been awarded the Distinguished Service Order (DSO) A very high award indeed, and rarely given to other than pilots. Once again the folk in the Dales towns of Richmond and Leyburn had reason to celebrate and feel proud. The Mayor of Richmond sent a third congratulatory letter on behalf of the people of Richmond and once again the local press made much of it. Not only did Alan receive a letter from the Mayor of Richmond; he also received a congratulatory letter from Air Vice Marshal Basil Embry the C in C. Embry not only congratulated Alan on the award; he also congratulated him on being one of only three Observers to be awarded the DSO so far in the war. A rare distinction indeed. The award of the DSO to Alan appeared in the London Gazette on the 19th of October 1943.

The citation read;

Flight Lieutenant John Alan Broadley. DFC DFM (47690) Royal Air Force 161 Squadron. Flight Lieutenant Broadley is a navigator of exceptional merit. He has completed a large number of sorties, rendering most valuable service and his efforts have contributed materially to the successes achieved.

This citation like the one for the DFC may seem to be a little sparing on the detail and his achievements, but that was due to the fact that almost all of his flying was top secret and therefore could not be mentioned. There was no doubt a lot of celebrating went in at the Mess that night, which was the usual thing whenever anyone was decorated. Whenever a serviceman is decorated he is almost always invited to Buckingham Palace to meet the Sovereign.

Borough of Richmond, Yorkshire.

Mayor's Parlour,
Town Hall,
Richmond, Yorkshire.

WR/JBK.

15th October, 1943.

Dear Flight Lieutenant Broadley,

It was only five months ago that I had the pleasure of sending you my congratulations on the award to you of the Distinguished Flying Cross, and now we have news that you have been awarded the Distinguished Service Order. This is a decoration which I, of my personal knowledge, know is awarded in really exceptional cases, and though I can only conjecture the feat of arms you must have performed to receive it, I know that it must have been for conspicuous gallantry. On my own behalf and on behalf of the townspeople of Richmond, I send you my sincere congratulations on this "treble event". Again, I wish you "Happy Landings" at all times.

Yours very sincerely,

W. Robinson

Mayor.

Flt. Lieut. J.A. Broadley, D.S.O., D.F.C., D.F.M.,
Officers' Mess,
Sculthorpe,
Fakenham.

The letter from the Mayor of Richmond on the award of the DSO

Headquarters, No. 2 Group,
Royal Air Force,
Bylaugh Hall,
Dereham,
Norfolk.

2G/BEE/DO.

6th October, 1943.

Dear Broadley,

I am writing to congratulate you most heartily on the award of the D.S.O. I cannot say how pleased I am over this latest recognition of your splendid work.

You now share, I believe I am correct in saying, the distinction of being one of the three Observers to win the D.S.O. in this war.

I should like to take this opportunity to tell you how welcome you are in this Group, and I look forward with confidence to the results of your combined team work with Group Captain Pickard.

Good show!

Yours sincerely

B.E. Embry.

Flight Lieutenant J. A. Broadley,
D.S.O., D.F.C., D.F.M.,
R.A.F. Station,
SCULTHORPE.

The letter from AVM Basil Embry on the award of the DSO.

CENTRAL CHANCERY OF
THE ORDERS OF KNIGHTHOOD.
ST JAMES'S PALACE, S.W.1.

12th November 1943

CONFIDENTIAL.

Sir,

The King will hold an Investiture at Buckingham Palace on Tuesday, the 23rd November, 1943, at which your attendance is requested.

It is requested that you should be at the Palace not later than 10.15 o'clock a.m.

DRESS-Service Dress, Morning Dress, Civil Defence Uniform or Dark Lounge Suit.

This letter should be produced on entering the Palace, as no further card of admission will be issued.

Two tickets for relations or friends to witness the Investiture may be obtained on application to this Office and you are requested to state your requirements on the form enclosed.

Please complete the enclosed form and return immediately to the Secretary, Central Chancery of the Orders of Knighthood, St. James's Palace, London, S.W.1.

I am, Sir,
Your obedient Servant,

Secretary.

Flight Lieutenant John A. Broadley,
D.S.O., D.F.C., D.F.M.

Alan's invitation to Buckingham Palace.

F 311309

ROYAL AIR FORCE

GOVERNMENT RAILWAY PASSENGER WARRANT

The railway warrant for Kitty to travel to Buckingham Palace.

Alan was no different and he duly received notice to attend the Palace for the 23rd of November to have the DSO pinned on his chest by His Majesty King George VI. He was allowed to take three guests so he invited his Aunt Peggy, Uncle jack and of course Kitty. When Kitty received her invitation to go to Buckingham Palace, her life went into somewhat of a whirl. Her first concern was what she might wear, a major concern even in wartime. The problem was solved when the Senior Student kindly loaned her a suit for the occasion. The train journey from North Wales to London thanks to the courtesy of an Air Ministry rail warrant was what she describes as the beginning of a dream. Arriving at Buckingham Palace she remembers that Alan seemed to be understandably quite nervous. The whole day and the events of the investiture remain a dream to this day, but without doubt, a wonderful experience. All to soon they both had to go their separate ways. After a fond farewell, Alan left to rejoin his squadron at Sculthorpe. Later when Alan came home on leave, his father constantly badgered him by asking how he had earned the DSO. All Alan could say was "Wait until the war is over Dad" He just was not allowed to tell anyone of his secret flying activities.

Back at Sculthorpe there began an intense period of low level flying and Gee training by the squadron which was broken by an interesting 1hr 40mins trip to RAF Lynham. It was interesting inasmuch that they had an extra passenger in their Mosquito. That passenger was Lord Londonderry a close family friend of the Pickards. It must be added that Ming was a passenger also. So Ming claimed more hours to be entered in her very her own Dog-logbook. The three of them brought Lord Londonderry back to Sculthorpe the next day. On the 2nd of December Alan and Pick prepared for their second operation in their Mosquito. The target was a group of barges at Cleve and Ijmuiden on the Rhine. The attack like the previous one was low level and fast. The results were the same and the damage to F-Freddie was almost the same. As they stayed low and banked for home, the aircraft shuddered as a burst of Flak hit it. Fortunately both engines responded well and they made it back to base fast and low without any further trouble. By now Alan and Pick were becoming more experienced in low level bombing attacks and this was to be the norm for the Squadron of 140 Wing. Pick although a peaceable man but one who revelled in the sheer danger and proximity to death, was reputed to have told a colleague over the telephone that, the sweat on his soaking shirt after returning from a low level raid was 'Worth a Guinea an ounce' True or not, that was the enthusiasm of Pick.

On the 4th of December there was for Alan and Kitty, a break from the tensions and worries of war when Alan plucked up the courage and wrote to ask Kitty if she would marry him. Kitty replied with a very prompt YES! and then added "With all my love" When Alan received her answer he replied saying that he felt more nervous waiting for her reply than he felt about flying on the low level sorties. He also added that he did not know when he would be able to get out to buy the ring as that there was a very important mission to be undertaken but the conditions had to be just right, but he held out hope for some leave at Christmas. The happiness and love felt by Kitty was twofold. Not only had Alan asked her if she would marry him, but he had proposed on her 21st Birthday. The following few days after the attack on Cleve, the weather deteriorated and all that could be carried out were short training exercises. However by the 21st the weather had cleared sufficiently for the Wing to resume its attacks. The Mosquitoes took off to attack Rocket Projectile Installations at St. Nicholas near Dieppe, but as they approached the target area, the weather deteriorated so badly they were compelled to return. Those rocket projectile installations were in fact V1 or 'Doodlebug' sites and posed a serious threat to the Allies and to the Home Counties whenever the invasion was to take place. Bomber Command first attacked rocket sites on the 16/17th August 1943 when 596 four engined bombers consisting of Lancasters, Halifaxes and Stirlings attacked Peenemunde on the Baltic coast. Their aim was to knock out the V1 and V2 Rocket Projectile Experimental Centre, and also to kill as many of the scientists and technical staff as possible. The raid was fairly successful, putting back the project by some three months, but 47 bombers were shot down chiefly to the 'Schrage Musik' armed night fighters that were used for the first time. The bomber losses would have been even greater but for a Mosquito diversionary raid to Berlin which drew away most of the fighters. Although the heavy bombers did a reasonable job, this did not stop the Germans from building up chain of V sites along the coastline. SOE agents in Holland and France supplied the British Military Intelligence with the locations and the numbers. Photographic Reconnaissance Unit (PRU) Spitfires obtained the photographs of the sites and installations. The task of knocking out as many of these sites as possible was given to the Mosquito Squadrons of No 2 Group. There was no time to be lost and on the 22nd of December the raid to St. Nicholas was on again and Air Vice Marshal Embry briefed the crews as to the exact and important nature of the raid. As previously arranged, Pick would lead the first wave and he (Embry) the second. The crews studied a model of the rocket site and familiarised themselves with the approach and exit areas keeping in mind all the Flak gun positions. After the final briefing they walked to their aircraft and prepared for take off. At 1040hrs forty eight Mosquitoes took off in pairs left and right of the runway at 75 yards separation and made formation and headed for France. They flew low level over the Channel to avoid the radar and raced into the rocket sites. They went into the attack at thirty feet and shattered the rocket site with deadly accurate bombing. This low level sortie was more successful than previous attacks and there was next to no casualties save for a few holes in the wings and fuselages plus shattered panels on the bombers due to colliding with seagulls and Flak splinters. They landed and almost immediately the Mosquitoes were refuelled, rearmed and bombed up for yet another crack at the same rocket site at St. Nicholas. A mere 2hrs after landing from the first bombing sortie, they were taking off again. The results were the same and the attack caught the German defences off guard. They returned to base at 1645hrs, having carried out two attacks in little more than four hours of flying. The Squadrons of 140 Wing were by now becoming very expert in the art of fast low level bombing, but Basil Embry knew that yet more training and operational sorties were needed to bring the Wing up to full offensive capability. He knew more than most that low level bombing although very effective was very dangerous and could be costly in crews and aircraft. The all pervading problem for this and other offensive flying was the weather and the weather in late December was not the best for low level operations.

21/12/43	0840	MOSQUITO HX. 922	G/C. PICKARD	— —	OPS. ST. NICHOLAS D'ALIERMONT RECALLED AT ENEMY COAST	2.10	
22/12/43	10.40	MOSQUITO HX. 922	G/C. PICKARD	— —	OPS. ST NICHOLAS. ROCKET PROJECTILE INSTALLATION. FORMATION LEADER	2.10	
22/12/43	1445	MOSQUITO HX. 922	G/C. PICKARD	— —	OPS. ST. NICHOLAS D'A. R.P.I	2.00	
29/12/43	1345	MOSQUITO SB-V	F/O ALEXANDER	— —	BASE — LEEMING	1.10	

The entry in Alan's logbook for the attacks on St. Nicholas.

However it was almost Christmas and leave for the festive season was hoped and longed for and the weather played its part in reducing flying conditions to almost zero. Alan applied and managed to get home on leave for the 24th and on Christmas Day Alan and Kitty announced their engagement. Always the ones not to make a fuss or to be in the headlines, they didn't publish the event in the local newspapers but just celebrated at home privately. A wonderful leave was enjoyed, but Alan had to say his farewells and left for his squadron. On the 29th of December Alan flew in his Mosquito to Leeming an RAF station in Yorkshire close to Richmond and so the New Year was seen in with Kitty and his friends. He returned to Sculthorpe and from their, 21 Squadron was moved to RAF Hunsdon in

readiness for a special operation. That special operation was the one he had mentioned some weeks earlier to Kitty although not in any great detail. The low level raids they had been doing, was all part of the preparations for that sortie. The weather continued to restrict flying, but on the 28th of January the weather cleared enough for another low level attack to be launched. The target was the V1 installation at Bois Coquerel. Once again the attack was a success and more low level experience was gained by Pick, Alan.
Time was drawing near for them to carry out that special operation, code, named…

Chapter Five

Operation Jericho

The Resistance Organisation in France in late 1943 although very successful, was continually being infiltrated and undermined by German counter espionage. As a result, hundreds of Resistance Workers had been arrested and thrown into the prison at Amiens in Picardy northern France. For the Allies, the situation was becoming desperate. The whole sabotage system run by the SOE and American OSS was beginning to crack and it was vital that the Underground Movement was kept as a viable proposition for the forthcoming invasion. Almost all of the Resistance Workers that had been captured were under the sentence of death and the Allies were laying plans in the November and December of that year to try and release them. Those plans were that a low level bombing raid attacking the prison walls to release those detained there should be attempted. They were the plans; the difficulty was how was it to be done? The AOC AVM Embry decided that he would lead the attack with Pick as his second in command. When the CinC heard of that part of the plan, he expressly forbade Embry to fly, he could not afford to lose such a senior officer. Embry argued that he had recently flown on previous low level sorties (under the pseudonym of 'Wing Commander Smith') but the C in C was unmoved. Embry had no choice and so the show was handed over to Pick. Embry admired Pick enormously, but was well aware that he had not carried out sufficient low level daylight raids to be certain of him being able to carry off this one and he was also well aware of Pick's impetuosity. Despite all the misgivings, the die had been cast and so it was Pick who was to lead. From then, all time and energy was put into the planning of Operation Jericho, the plan to blow down the walls and free some 700 prisoners within. The operation was originally code named Operation Renovate but was changed to Jericho for very obvious reasons and it was to take place sooner rather than later. Six aircraft from No 487 (RNZAF) 464 (RAAF) and 21 (RAF) Squadrons would carry out the bombing with a Film Unit Mosquito to record the action. There was to be a fighter escort from Nos., 174, 245 and 198 Typhoon Squadrons. On the 8th of February right in the middle of all this planning and secrecy, Alan reached his 23rd birthday but there was no time to celebrate, the show had to go on. The original attack was to take place on the 10th of February, but the atrocious weather continued and so postponement was the only option. The

High Command was becoming increasingly anxious. Time it seemed was not on the side of the RAF and most definitely not on the side of the French people inside the prison at Amiens. Execution day was drawing ever near and if the Germans had so much as a whiff of the impending raid the death sentences would be carried out very swiftly. As the weather deteriorated the anxiety of the 'Brass' increased. On the 17th the Met reports gave little hope of any improvement. On the 18th Embry ordered the crews to report for a brief on the raid, saying that if there was so much as break in the weather the raid was on, it was to be then or never and never was not an option. The crews entered the briefing room and were addressed by Embry who explained what exactly was expected of them. Until that moment, the only people who knew the precise nature of the raid were Embry and Pick. After Embry's brief, Pick unveiled a wooden mock up model of Amiens prison. All the crews studied it and took notes. Although Pick and Alan were part of No 21 Squadron. they were to fly in the last aircraft of 464 Squadron, this was to allow Pick to make an assessment of the results. The attack plan was for 487 Squadron to bomb the outer walls and the German guardroom as the timing of the attack was when the Germans might be expected to be having their mid-day meal in their Mess. 464 Squadron was to breach the actual prison walls, thus allowing the prisoners to break free. The third squadron No 21 was to be held in reserve and their task was to bomb the whole area if the breach had not been made, in reality to kill the inmates before the Germans could take their revenge. All were agreed that the chaps flying in 21 Squadron had the most onerous task of all. If the raid was deemed to be a failure, that is if the prisoners were not seen to be escaping, 21 Squadron was to bomb. The French partisans who were being held in the prison who were facing death by many forms of execution, had let it be known that they preferred to die by RAF bombs than at the hands of the Gestapo. The French also accepted that a great many would die even if the raid were successful. The crews of 21 Squadron were aghast at the thought of having to kill those gallant French partisans, but that was the task and they accepted it. Pick was not too pleased about having to make the decision of whether the first bombing waves had been successful or not. If they were not, he was to say of the W/T 'GREEN-GREEN GREEN!' If they were successful he was to say 'RED-RED-RED!' As the crews continued the familiarisation of the model, Embry spoke once again and emphasised the importance of success. There would not be another chance so everyone had to do the job first time as news had filtered through from the Resistance that the execution day for the prisoners was set for the 19th of February. That then was the reality of the task that lay ahead for those thirty six airmen. The Intelligence Officer warned of the Flak positions around the target and of the 'Abbeville Boys' a famous German fighter unit operating the superb Focke Wulf 190 close to the town of Amiens commanded by the redoubtable Adolf Galland. The fact that there was a crack German fighter base close to Amiens was very carefully noted. The heavy and predictable Flak was one thing, but the Focke Wulf 190 fighters was another. The closing words of briefing uttered by Pick were "Well boys this is a death or glory show. If you never do anything else you can still count this as the finest job you could have ever done." Prophetic words indeed! The crews rose and walked to their Messes for a meal and waited for the Met report. The Met report came through, things were not improving by any great margin, but there was just a chance. By 10.00hrs there had been no improvement but there was a chance of brighter weather across the Channel. Each was left with his own thoughts. By 10.00hrs the weather had improved very slightly and they were ordered to report to their squadrons. So the decision had been made. Bad weather or not, Pick had decided that the show was on, there could be no more delay. He spoke to the RAF Film Unit crew and told them that he would be orbiting the target and said, "Should anything happen to me, I would like you to take over and assess whether the raid has been successful or not" The two film crew nodded their reluctant agreement. No one it seemed wanted to take on the responsibility of sending in the third wave. The Mosquitoes were given a final detailed preparation and check for this very special low level attack, then crews climbed aboard.

With thundering engines eighteen Mosquitoes rolled down the runway, the mist and the snow swirling around each aircraft. They headed south where they were to rendezvous with their fighter escort of Typhoons from No's 174,198 and 245 Squadrons. When they reached the rendezvous point they couldn't see each other let alone the typhoons, the sky was so black and murky. Four of the Mosquitoes became hopelessly lost and tried to get back to Hunsdon leaving fourteen aircraft for the raid. Of the twelve escorting Typhoons, four had also became lost; it was not a good start. Undismayed the remainder flew low across the Channel where they ran into perfect visibility and onward to the Somme region of France and then on to Amiens. The run into Amiens was along the Albert-Amiens from the east. This very straight road led to the town and directly to the prison. As the attacking force prepared for the bombing run, by now down to twelve Mosquitoes as two of 21s had also been forced to return, the Flak that greeted them was extremely accurate and dense. One of the leading Mosquitoes of 464 Squadron became a casualty well before the target had been reached when its port engine began trailing smoke. The pilot Flt/Lt 'Tich' Hanafin feathered the propeller of the engine and attempted to keep going to the target. The Mossie responded well but within sight of the target the engine began to vibrate badly. Not wanting to jeopardise the timing of the attack he pulled clear and dropped his bombs in open country, and headed back to England. Then a burst of Flak hit the aircraft and a splinter embedded itself deep into his neck causing paralysis. The wound began bleeding profusely and he began to lose consciousness. His navigator, P/O Redgrave, propped him up and gave him a shot of morphine and between them they managed to fly the damaged Mosquito back towards England finally making a safe landing at a fighter airfield in Sussex. In the meantime, the five remaining bombers of the first wave of the New Zealanders led by Kiwi 'Black' Smith, an ex Battle of Britain pilot, was heading for the prison. Three went straight in and bombed with their eleven second delay fused bombs, the other two made a feint over the railway station to allow the delay fuses to operate. They went in and dropped their bombs and peeled away, W/C Smith dropping his bombs from a height of just 10 feet. The Australians led by W/C Bob Iredale came in fast. Realising that the bombs had not yet exploded he led his aircraft into a 360 degree turn which took them over Glisy airfield. The Flak soon greeted them and got their range, but more ominously the 'Abbeville Boys' were taking off in their yellow nosed Focke Wulf 190 fighters. After the bombs from the New Zealanders exploded the debris and smoke had hardly time to settle before the four mosquitoes of the Australian Squadron came boring in. In the meantime, the Typhoons were circling the Abbeville airfield waiting for the scrambling German fighters. The New Zealanders had achieved what they set out to do, that is to breach the outer walls. It was up to the Aussie Squadron to breach the prison walls. In the last of those Mossies were Pick and Alan. By the time F-Freddie had gone into the bombing run, they were travelling very low and very fast. Alan dropped the bombs with the yell 'Bombs Gone! and they climbed skywards. After the timed delay, they saw the walls of the prison collapse with smoke and debris billowing skywards. The Mossies in front of Pick and Alan banked and set course for home. Pick kept F-Freddie climbing to five hundred feet and then he orbited the area and he began to make his assessment of the damage done which would allow him to decide the next course of action. What Pick and Alan saw, were scores and scores of people running out of the broken down walls. The ones that flung themselves flat when the bombers came over were the Germans, the ones that kept running, were the prisoners, escape was their sole aim. In the meantime the Mosquito of the RAF Film Unit was also orbiting and filming those epic and dramatic events. Pick had one more look at the scene below and then called to the leader of 21 Squadron, W/C Dale and said in a loud and clear but calm voice RED-RED-RED. W/C Dale didn't need a second reminder; he banked his aircraft and headed for home, followed by the much relieved crews of the squadron. Pick satisfied that the show was over began his turn for home. It was then that he saw a Mosquito that was obviously in trouble after being hit by Flack. He banked F-Freddie round and went to investigate the stricken bomber to check if the crew might bale out. In that Mosquito was pilot S/Ldr McRitchie and his navigator Flt/Lt Sampson. A burst of Flak had exploded close to the aircraft killing Sampson instantly and paralysing McRitchie down one side of his body. The Mosquito was badly damaged and began to go out of control. Struggling with the controls by the use of one hand, McRitchie managed to keep it flying straight and level and succeeded in carrying out a crash landing on a snow covered field at more than 200mph. The force of the impact flung him clear but without suffering any further injury.

As Pick and Alan watched the progress of the stricken Mosquito, two Focke Wulf 190 fighters of the 'Abbeville Boys' pounced. They dived from the advantage of altitude, the only way a FW190 could out pace a Mosquito, and began their attack. There is speculation that there was a dogfight with the two Germans taking on F-Freddie. There is also speculation that Pick's Mossie had been damaged by Flak thus making it more difficult to manoeuvre. The result of the combat was that the tail of Alan and Pick's Mosquito was shot away causing the aircraft to cartwheel and crash onto the snow covered ground near St. Gratien, a village but a few kilometres from Amiens. With no chance of being able to use their parachutes;

Flight Lieutenant Alan 'Bill' Broadley DSO DFC DFM and Group Captain Charles 'Pick' Pickard DSO DFC died.**

Thus bringing to an end one of the most remarkable air combat partnerships in the annals of the Royal Air Force.

Chapter Six
Finale

Consternation was growing at Hunsdon. All but two of the Mosquitoes that attacked had returned to England, if not back to Hunsdon. Almost all the Mosquitoes had suffered Flak damage and apart from Alan and Pick, there was one other crew missing. McRitchie and Sampson. It was later learnt that after crashing, McRitchie was taken to a French hospital and then onto a POW camp, Sampson who had died in the attack was buried near where he fell. Back at Hunsdon, each man in the squadron was convinced that Alan and Pick would make it back, it was inconceivable that the great team would not do so. But they weren't to return. Dorothy Pickard who was told later that evening that Charles was missing replied "Pick is dead" She knew it and so did faithful Ming, who whined and whimpered most of the night.

At the time of the dogfight between F-Freddie and the two FW 190's a cluster of French Peasants were watching the proceedings with overawed interest. When they saw the Mosquito crash, they hurried to the scene and began extricating the two dead flyers. They wrapped them in their parachutes and carried them to the Mayor's house in St. Gratien. One French girl had the presence of mind to cut away the flying wings, decorations and rank markings of Alan and Pick thus denying the Germans the knowledge of whom they had shot down. Despite their efforts, and before they had chance to bury the two airmen, a group of German soldiers arrived and took the bodies away. Once again with commendable quick thinking, one of the French partisans gouged four grooves into the top of Alan Broadley's coffin, to allow it to be identified from that of Pick's when the time came for them to be given a proper burial.

Without doubt Operation Jericho was a spectacular success. Although scores of French patriots and ordinary French people died in the attack, more than 250 survived including twelve who were due to be shot the next day. Not only did Patriots escape, many common criminals escaped also. The Partisans who escaped retained their liberty till the end of the war and continued working for and with the Allies. In that context the raid on Amiens prison was in every way worthwhile. The stunning success of the attack was the precursor to several more low level Mosquito raids, notably the attack on the Philips factory in The Hague and on the Gestapo Headquarters in Copenhagen.

In the twin Yorkshire market towns of Leyburn and Richmond, the news filtered through that Alan Boadley had been reported missing. This was confirmed by the usual Air Ministry telegrams to Alan's father and his Aunt Peggy. There was nothing to say what had happened or whether he had been taken Prisoner of War. At the Teacher Training College at Borth in North Wales, Kitty Ovesby received the news with a sense of loneliness and over powering sadness. Like many more anxious mothers, fathers, wives and girl friends of those times, Kitty realised that she was in no position to be thought of as any different, but despite this, the sadness and shock was hardly bearable. Alan had been reported missing before and had he not returned safely? He would do so again she reasoned. She simply hung onto the belief that Alan was safe and that one day, he would return. Although the staff and the other girls at the college were genuinely sympathetic and rallied round, Kitty didn't have the comfort of her family and friends who were all far away in Yorkshire. Loneliness accompanied her grief. Kitty kept herself control and concentrated on her studies as the qualifying examinations were due the coming summer. Sometime later she wrote to the Officer Commanding Alan's Squadron asking if they might return the ring that he had bought for their engagement. The reply she received was chilling. They wrote in a matter of fact way, stating that 'Alan's room had been sealed as per regulations, but if anything was found they would forward it on to her' No offer of sympathy, no offer of hope-nothing. Kitty felt a wave of bitterness but there was nothing for her to do but to carry on the best she could. During her Easter holiday in Richmond, a sergeant of No 487 Squadron Royal New Zealand Air Force arrived to see Kitty. He brought with him a ring set with an emerald surrounded by tiny diamonds, it was the ring that Alan had bought earlier in the year. The sergeant asked Kitty if she thought that Alan was still alive, She replied saying that she believed he was. He made no comment and Kitty was too fearful to ask what he thought or knew. From that day, Kitty wore Alan's ring as her talisman, a reminder of the love and friendship they both shared. The summer passed and there was still no news. Kitty was by now in the final term of her training course and exams were looming, and she had to travel up to London for her final physiotherapy examination. She confesses that she remembers very little of the exam, but she does recall hearing the song of the cuckoos in the suburban gardens. In her own words, she thought she must have been running on 'automatic pilot' as she passed the exams with no real problems. By this time the Invasion of North West Europe had taken place and there was a surge of hope within the whole nation. Kitty still clung to her belief that Alan and Pick were safe somewhere and she reasoned that if they weren't, why had not the Air Ministry announced it?

After successfully qualifying, Kitty applied for a post as a PE teacher at Saltburn High School in North Riding of Yorkshire. She was accepted and was to take up her position in the September. Arriving at the High School she was confronted by a most unprepossessing building which was far too small and as a result, had been surrounded by a batch of temporary classrooms. The school may have been a disappointment for Kitty, but the girls were wonderful. She found them to be warm hearted, generous and independent of spirit who put their heart and soul into everything.

In her digs one morning while having breakfast, Kitty picked up the Daily Mail and the stark headlines stared out at her,

'AMIENS PRISON RAID'.

The headline went on to give an account of the prison break out by the French Patriots after the walls had been blown down by the Mosquitoes. Then it told of Mosquito F-Freddie being shot down with the loss of Alan and Pick. On reading those words the shock felt by Kitty was horrendous. Reading about it in a daily newspaper ended all the months of hoping and waiting. The Landlady of the digs realising that Kitty could not possibly go to the school that day sent a note to the Headmistress explaining the situation and stayed to comfort her. Sometime later, Kitty 's aunt from Richmond arrived at the digs. She had hoped to get over to see Kitty before the newspapers had been delivered, but she was too late. So Kitty had finally learnt of the fate of Alan Broadley, the boy from the Dales. A boy who with rare but quiet courage and an enigmatic smile. She knew life was to change and that life had to go on, so she put all her thoughts and energies into the school, her schoolwork and the scholars.

Apparently Pick had talked with Alan of what he might do after the war. Pick himself had ideas of staying in aviation and flying in the Colonies. He asked if Alan if he might consider being a partner. Kitty is sure that Alan would have gone with Pick with hardly a second thought, but their dreams were never to be fulfilled.

Some years after the war Kitty met Randell Jeffery who, in her own words was and is 'A kind and understanding man' who like Alan had witnessed the vicissitudes of war at first hand. Rendall had escaped from Dunkirk, served in North Africa and Italy and like Kitty, he was a schoolteacher. They married in 1954 and now have three children, Clare, Nicholas and Katherine. Kitty and Randell now live in retirement in the south of England.

When Pick and Alan were re-interred at St. Pierre after the war, the local people painted on the wooden cross of Pick's grave the inscription;

Group Captain Pickard. VC DSO DFC.

The investing of the VC was genuine mistake. The problem of how to have the VC inscription removed without embarrassing the local people was solved when Dorothy Pickard requested they should have it changed. Both Alan and Pick had a wooden cross placed above their graves in the early days after the war, but now they have the Commonwealth War Graves Commission. Head Stone in place of those wooden crosses.

On the Sunday nearest to the anniversary of the Amiens raid, the local people hold a memorial service in Amiens Cathedral after which there is a wreath laying ceremony at the cemetery at St.Pierre, the final resting place for Alan and Pick. Dorothy Pickard the widow of Pick attended these ceremonies until ill health prevented her from travelling from her home in South Africa. Dorothy Pickard died in March 1999.

So ended the story of a young Yorkshireman and his inseparable Skipper and friend Charles Pickard. They both fought for their country, both were highly decorated and both paid the ultimate price. Alan Broadly may well have been destined for a higher rank in the RAF than he attained, but that would have ensured that he did not fly on so many operations. He would no doubt have eschewed that opportunity to do what he knew he could do best-navigate an aeroplane against the enemy. For his service to his country and bravery in action,

Alan Broadley was awarded the;

Distinguished Service Order
Distinguished Flying Cross
Distinguished Flying Medal
1939-45 Star
Aircrew Europe Star
Defence Medal
War Medal

Alan Broadley is remembered on the War Memorial in Leyburn, the Parish Church in Leyburn, Richmond Grammar School, on the Richmond War Memorial and in The Central Church of the Royal Air Force St. Clement Danes London and at St. Pierre France.

On the 5th of December 1944, a grateful nation held a Memorial Service to the memory Alan and Charles at St. Martin in the Field London.

Inscribed on the Headstone of Alan's grave at St. Pierre, are the words;

'All that he came to give, he gave and went again'

The Mosquito Squadrons on Operation Jericho
18th February 1944.

487 Squadron (RNZAF)

Pilot	Navigator
W/C Smith DFC	Flt/Lt Barnes.DFM
F/S Jennings	W/O Nichols
P/O Sparks	P/O Dunlop
P/O Darrel	P/O Stevenson
P/O Fowler	P/O Wilkins
Flt/Lt Hanafin	P/O Redgrave

464 Squadron (RAAF)

W/C Iredale DFC	F/L McCAul DFC
S/L Sugden	F/O Bridger
F/O Monaghan DFM	FLt/Lt Dean DFC
Flt/Lt McPhee DFM	Flt/Lt Atkins
S/L Ritchie	F/L Sampson
G/C Pickard DSO**DFC	Flt/Llt Broadley DSO DFC DFM

21 Squadron (RAF)

W/C Dale	P/O Gabites
Flt/Lt Benn DFC	F/O Roe
Flt/L Wheeler DFC	F/O Redington
F/Lt Taylor DFC	S/L Livery-Level DFC (FFAF)
Flt/Lt Hogan	F/S Crowfoot
F/S Steadman	P/O Reynolds

RAF Film Unit Mosquito.

Flt/Lt Wickham	P/O Howard

Typhoons from 174, 198 and 245 Squadrons as fighter escort.

'And it shall come to pass, that when they make a long blast with their ram's horns, and when ye hear the sound of the trumpet, all the people shall shout with a great shout; and the wall of the city shall fall down flat, and the people shall ascend up, every man straight before him'

(Joshua)

Time carried forward:— 664·40 396·

JANUARY 1944.

Date	Hour	Aircraft Type and No.	Pilot	Duty	Remarks (including results of bombing, gunnery, exercises, etc.)	Flying Times Day	Flying Times Night
28/1/44	[illegible]	MOSQUITO HX. 922	G/C. PICKARD	NAVIGATOR F/LT. A. BROADLEY	OPS. R.P.I. – BOIS COQUEREL	2·05	
FEBRUARY 1944							
2/2/44	1200	MOSQUITO [illegible] 410	G/C. PICKARD	NAVIGATOR F/LT. A. BROADLEY	BASE – LYNEHAM – BASE.	1·24	

KILLED IN ACTION

FEB 18th 1944 AMIENS.

CENTRAL DEPOSITORY · JUL 1946 · ROYAL AIR FORCE

The final entry in Alan's logbook.

Unit	From	To	Unit	From	To
[illegible] Aux. Sqdn Usworth.	[illegible]/6/39	[illegible]/8/39			
No 215 (B) Sqdn Honington (Suffolk)	[illegible]/8/39	[illegible]/9/39			
215 (B) Sqdn. [illegible]	[illegible]/9/39	22/9/39			
215 (B) Bassingbourn	[illegible]/9/39	[illegible]/[illegible]/39			
[illegible] Sqn. Feltwell	30/11/39	[illegible]/1/40			
[illegible] Sqdn Stradishall	[illegible]/[illegible]/40	[illegible]/3/40			
99 Sqdn Newmarket	[illegible]/3/40	[illegible]/9/40			
20 O.T.U. Lossiemouth	[illegible]/9/40	[illegible]			
[illegible] Sqdn. [illegible]	[illegible]	[illegible]			
[illegible] Flt. Newmarket	[illegible]	[illegible]			
[illegible] Sqdn. [illegible]	[illegible]	[illegible]			
[illegible]	[illegible]	[illegible]			
[illegible] St Eval	1/8/[illegible]	[illegible]			
[illegible] Sqdn Tempsford	[illegible]	[illegible]			
[illegible]	[illegible]/[illegible]/43				

Type	Type
Avro Anson Mono. 2 Cheetah IX Eng.	Pratt & Whitney Engines Douglas "Havoc"
Fairey "Seal"	Mosquito Mk. VI 2 [illegible]
Overstrand	
Hawker "Hart"	
[illegible] 4 Pratt & Whitney [illegible]	
Handley Page "[illegible]"	
Vickers "Wellington" I 2 [illegible] Engines	
Vickers "Wellington" I[illegible]	
Vickers "Wellington" I[illegible]	
Vickers Wellington Mk II (Merlins)	
Whitley Mk [illegible] 2 R.R. Merlins	
Miles "Mentor"	
Vega Gull	
Hudson I & II	
Halifax V	
Westland Lysander	
Lockheed Ventura	
Oxford	

A list of all the squadrons and units where Alan was based and types of aircraft in which he flew.

THE COMPOSTELLAN

Vol. IX. July, 1937 No. 12.

—o—

SCHOOL OFFICERS.

Captain of the School:

F. H. Pedley.

—

School Prefects

F. H. Pedley (F). R. L. Wilkin (F)

House Prefects:

Watson R. M. (F) Hardman B. M. (G) Stephenson J. R. (S)
Best A. G. (F) Bell R. D. (G) Wylam J. H. (S)
Woolass G. L. (F) Carr T. (G)

—

Games Committee:

President	-	The Headmaster.
Captain	-	R. L. Wilkin.
Hon. Treas.	-	Mr. J. Pattern.
Hon. Sec.	-	T. A. Carr.
Mr. H. R. Vernon.		Mr. C. O. H. Worrall.

—

Editor of the Compostellan:

Mr. E. Bush.

Richmond Grammar School Magazine.

The Unveiling and Dedication

of

A Memorial

To those Old Boys of Richmond School who gave their lives in the 1939—1945 War

The Memorial, consisting of a Brass Tablet somewhat similar to those already in Big School commemorating the South African and 1914-1918 Wars, bears the Names of 29 Old Boys who gave their lives, and is the gift of the Old Boys' Association, which has also defrayed the cost of one of the Panels in the Richmond Memorial in the Parish Church

---

Sunday, 6th November, 1949

In Memoriam

1939—1945

—

DAVID HENRY ATKINSON.

JOHN McKENZIE SINCLAIR BAIN.

CHARLES GUTHRIE SHIELDS BAIN.

RAISBECK DENNIS BELL.

HENRY WILFRED ARTHUR BRITTON.

JOHN ALAN BROADLEY.

MATTHEW BRODERICK CHERRY.

RAYMOND COATES.

JOHN CRAVEN.

CHRISTOPHER DOUGLAS CURTIS.

THOMAS HARLAND DUCK.

JOHN LAWRENCE FOSTER.

WALTER GIBSON.

GEORGE ERIC JOHNSON.

JOHN THOMAS JOPLING.

LEONARD VINCENT KING.

FRANK EBRAY LAWSON.

ARTHUR MAWSON.

KENNETH WILLIAM MORTON.

MICHAEL KENNY PENDLEBURY.

WILLIAM THOMAS PEVERELL.

JOHN VERNON PROSSER.

LEONARD SCOTT.

THOMAS ROY SHAW.

GEORGE ERIC FITZGERALD SHUTE.

PHILIP GRANT SPENCER.

PETER SQUIRES.

JOHN REGINALD STEPHENSON.

ROBERT MACKINNON WATSON.

Richmond School
Yorkshire

Active Service Roll

July 1945

RICHMOND SCHOOL, YORKSHIRE
ACTIVE SERVICE ROLL
July 1945.

Adamson, P. H., 41-44, A.C., R.A.F.
Allen, A. D., 32-35, W.O., R.A.F.
Armstrong, J., 36-40, Pte., Parachute Regt.
Atkinson, C. R., 29-34, Sergeant, R.A.F.
Atkinson, D. H., 29-39, Flying Officer, R.A.F., killed in action.

Bailes, J., 29-33, Flying Officer, R.A.F.
Bailes, W. D., 33-36, Sergeant, R.A.F.
Bain, C. G. S., 29-36, Flight Lieut., R.A.F., killed in action.
Bain, F., 34-40, Captain, Gurkha Rifles.
Bain, J. McK. S., 29-36, Major, Cameron Highlanders, killed in action.
Bainbridge, J. J., 34-36, L.A.C., R.A.F,
Bainbridge, T. P., 37-42, Pte., R.A.M.C.
Balmain, J. J., 31-34, Lieut., R. Signals.
Bannochie, J. M. (Master), 35-40, Lieut., R.N.V.R.
Barker, G. A., 31-35, Lieut., R. Signals.
Barker, L., 33-37, Sergeant, R.A.F., Ex-P.O.W.
Barras, E. L., 34-40, Trooper, R.T.R.
Bartle, W. F., 33-35, L.A.C., R.A.F.
Bathurst, D. J., 33-35, Trooper, Inns of Court Regt.
Baynes, G., 31-37, Flying Officer, R.A.F., D.F.C., D.F.M.
Baynes, R. W., L/Corporal, R.A.C.
Baxter, J., 1924, Sergeant, R.A.F.
Bell, R. D., 31-39, Flight-Lieut., R.A.F., killed in action.
Best, A. G., 30-37, Major, Green Howards.
Best, C. M., 34-42, Midshipman, Merchant Navy.
Beverley, L. E., 35-36, Lieut., R.E.

Binks, E. W., 36-40, Sergeant-Pilot, R.A.F.

Blades, K. D., 38-44, Pte., G.S.C.

Blagdon, G., 30-31, Captain, Durham L.I.

Bland, C. L., 30-37, A.B., Merchant Navy, discharged (ill-health).

Bland, P. W. H. R., 30-35, Corporal, R.A.F.

Boland, C. H., 29-34, Major, A.A.P.C.

Bolton, J. W., 26-31, Craftsman, R.E.M.E.

Bolton, W. T. O., 25-31, Pte., R. Sussex Regt.

Borrows, H. R., 36-43, Pte., R.A.M.C.

Borrows, S., 30-35, Sergeant, R.A.F.

Bracey, K., 1917, Lieut., D.L.I.

Britton, H. W. R., 34-36, Pilot Officer, R.A.F., killed in action.

Broadley, J. A., 34-38, Flight Lieut., R.A.F., D,S,O., D.F.C., D.F.M., killed in action.

Brotherton, S., 27-31, Craftsman, R.E.M.E., discharged (ill health).

Brown, C. V., 30-34, Signalman, R. Signals.

Brown, E. D., 26-30, Captain, Merchant Navy.

Brown, E. M., 19-23, R.A.F.

Brown, R. C., 37-41, O/Sig., R.N.

Bullard, C., 16-18, Brigadier, R.E.M.E., C.B.E.

Burns, R. R. S., 34-38, Flight Sergeant, R.A.F.

Calvert, J. R., 32-38, Corporal, R.A.F.

Calvert, W. J., 35-41, Flying Officer, R.A.F.

Calvert, P. W., 12-16, Captain, Merchant Navy.

Campbell, P. E., 33-35, Major, Baluch Regt., prisoner of war.

Campbell, P. W. E., 1921, Captain, R.E.

Campbell, T. E., 1921, Major, I.A.O.C.

Cansdale, H. E., 39-45, Pte., G.S.C.

Carr, T., 31-39, Sub.-Lieut., R.N.V.R.

Carter, A. W., 31-36, Corporal, Royal Signals.

Carter, G. H., 30-33, Pilot Officer, R.A.F.

Cherry, M. B., 29-34, Chief Radio Officer, Merchant Navy, missing, believed drowned.

Cherry, W., 34-38, Corporal, R.A.F.

Clark, D. A. (Master), 36-   , Flying Officer, R.A.F.
Clark, J., 35-40, Petty Officer, Fleet Air Arm.
Clarke, E. C., 33-43, Lieut., 1/15th Punjab Regt.
Clarkson, T. W., 25-28, Major, R.A.
Clayden, C. N., 29-31, Captain, Middlesex Regt.
Climie, A., 31-35, Corporal, R.A.F.
Climie R., 29-31, Corporal, R.A.F.
Clitheroe, T., 30-36, Lieut., R.A. (A.A.)
Clynes, P. H., 33-35, Corporal, R.A.F.
Clynes, G. E, 33-35, Driver, R.A.S.C. (A.D.)
Coates, A., 28-32, Flight Lieut., R.A.F.
Coates, A. T., 29-32, L.A.C., R.A.F.
Coates, J. R., 30-32, Flight Lieut., R.A.F., D.F.C.,
Mentioned in Despatches.
Coates, R., 20-24, Sergeant, R.A.F., killed in action.
Coates, T. B., 31-37, Sergeant, R.A.F.
Coleby, A. S., 39-43, A.C., R.A.F.
Collinson, F. J., 29-33, Lieut., R.A.
Cooke, V., 31-35, C.S.M., Royal Signals.
Cooper, A. G. R., 30-33, Corporal, R.E.M.E.,
Mentioned in Despatches.
Cousans, S. D., 29-33, Captain, R.E.
Coyle, N. H., 24-28, Captain, R.W. Kent Regt.,
prisoner of war, repatriated (ill health).
Cradock, N., 23-26, Sergeant, A.M.P.C.
Cradock, P., 30-35, S.Q.M.S., R.E.M.E.
Craven, J., 34-39, Corporal, Royal Hussars,
killed in action.
Crofton, C. N., 31-34, Flight Sergeant, R.A.F.
Crofton, N. K., 24-31, Captain, R.E.
Cubberley, J. R., 33-40, Lieut., Royal Signals.
Curtis, C. D., 29-32, Flying Officer, R.A.F.,
died on active service.

Danby, R., 35-39, Sergeant, R.A.F.
D'Arcy, N. J. H., 10-13, Commander (E), R.N.
Davis, J. G. (Master), 33-34, Group Captain, R.A.F.,
O.B.E., Mentioned in Despatches.
Dickinson, F. (Master), 35—, Captain, Royal Signals.

Dobson, R., 38-42, Driver, R.A.S.C.
Done, J. E., 30-33, Sergeant, R.A.S.C.
Douglas, J. R., 39-40, Lieut., Royal Marines.
Downie, B., - , Commander, R.N.
Duck, T. H., 30-32, Gunner, R.A., killed in action.
Dugdale, J. L., 36-43, Private, R.A.S.C.
Duffield, E. F., 39-40, Private, R.A.O.C.

Elenor, R. W., 38-43, Cadet, Merchant Navy.
Evans, J. N., 31-32, Sergeant, R.A.F.
Eyles, D., 29-35, Bdr., R.A.(A.A.)

Ferguson, R. G., 38-43, Royal Marines.
Fergusson, J. C., 06-13, Major, Indian Army.
Finucane, A. M., 33-38, Lieut., Green Howards.
Finucane, L. R., 37-43, Midshipman (A), F.A.A.
Firby, J. B., 26-32, Sub. Lieut., R.N.V.R.
Foss, G. H. (Master), 33-35, Group Captain, R.A.F., O.B.E.(Mil.)
Foster, F. R., 30-33, Wing Commander, R.A.F.
Foster, J. L., 34-36, Flying Officer, R.A.F., killed in action.
Fry, G. P., 08-11, Purser, Merchant Navy.
Fryer, L. H., 22-26, Corporal, R.E.M.E.
Fryer, W., 23-24, L/Corporal, R.A.S.C.

Gadsby, R. T., 31-40, Lieut., K.R.I. Hussars.
Gaine, J. H., 32-39, Lieut., R.E.
Gaine, W. W., 1932, 2nd Officer, Merchant Navy.
Galaher, H. F. L., 26-28, Captain, R.A.M.C.
Gall, C. A., 22-27, Lieut., R.A.
Garget, J. R. B., 30-36, Corporal, R.A.S.C.
Gelber, H. G. V. E., 2nd Lieut., I.T.C.
Gibson, A., 32-37, L.A.C., R.A.F.
Glover, G., 34-39, Flight Lieut., R.A.F.
Goulding, J. W., 25-29, Captain, Merchant Navy.
Groves, J. H., 31-36, Captain, R.A.S.C.
Groves, S. N., 34-39, L.A.C., R.A.F.
Guy, R. J., 32-34, Driver, R.A.S.C.

Haigh, A. D., 29-33, Corporal, R.E.
Hall, J. G., 35-38, Ldg. Seaman, R.N.
Hall, T. N., 30-33, Sgt. Pilot, R.A.F.
Hallowes, R. B., 30-35, Sub. Lieut., R.N.
Halstead, H. F., 32-36, Flying Officer, R.A.F.
Hammond, R., 30-33, Petty Officer, R.N.
Hancock, J. H., 33-36, Lieut., K.O.Y.L.I.,
resigned Commission (ill health).
Hannay, L. V., 28-31, Sergeant, R.A.F. Regt.
Hardman, C. D., 33-39, Sapper, R.E.,
discharged (ill health).
Hardman, B. M., 29-37, Private, Green Howards.
Harker, G. F., 30-35, Captain, R.A.Ch.D.
Harrison, A. B., 36-39, Captain, Ghurka Rifles.
Haynes, J. W., 34-40, L.A.C., R.A.F.
Hayward, G. R. S., 23-26, Gunner, R.A.
Helme, T. A., 38-41, Private, R.A.S.C.
Hemstock, J., 26-30, Corporal, Royal Signals.
Henwood, L. J., 39-42, Sgmn., Royal Signals.
Henwood, P., 39-42, Lieut., R.E.
Heseltine, S., 35-40, Trooper, R.A.C.
Heseltine, W., 34-40, Corporal, R.A.C.
Heslop, H. W., O.B.E., 09-13, T/Air Commodore, R.A.F.
Hetherington, R. A., 36-41, Lieut., R.E.
Hewitt, R. K., 28-30, Flight Lieut., R.A.F., C.G.M.,
D.F.M.
Hicks, E. W., 35-42, Sapper, R.E.
Hird, A., 35-42, A.C., R.A.F.
Hird, J. R., 31-36, Sergeant, C.M.P.
Hodgson, F. C., 16-23, A.C., R.A.F.,
discharged (ill health).
Hodgson, J., 35-40, Capt., 13th Frontier Force Rifles.
Hodgson, L. W., 29-33, Sergeant, R.A.M.C.
Holmes, A. N. C., 35-41, Corporal, Royal Signals.
Holmes, G. B., 34-39, L/Corporal, Reconnaissance Regt.
Holmes, I. S., 26-33, Capt., R.A.
Holwill, P. K., 39-41, Sub. Lieut., R.N.V.R.
Holywell, J., 32-36, Flight Lieut., R.A.F.

Hopkins, D. E., 37-43, L.R.M., R.N.

Hopkinson, W. A., 29-34, Captain,
Duke of Wellington's Regt.

Horner, C. W., 25-33, Lieut., Worcestershire Regt.

Howell, P. J., 31-37, Major, Green Howards.

Huck, J. V., 19-23, Sergeant, Essex Regt.

Hughes, A. W., 37-40, Private, Canadian Army.

Hunt, I. A., 32-36, Corporal, R.E.M.E.

Hunter, D. J., 31-36, L.A.C., R.A.F.

Hunter, K. W., 36-41, Cadet, R.A.F.

Husband, G. A., 20-25, A.F., R.N.

Husband, W. H., 19-24, Gunner, R.A.

Hutchinson, J. S., - , Trooper, R.T.R.

Hutchinson, W., 29-32, Flight Lieut., R.A.F., D.F.C.

Inness, W. I. C., 28-34, Group Capt., R.A.F.,
Mentioned in Despatches.

Jackson, A., 31-36, Sergeant, R.A.F.

Jeffrie, A. B., 38-42, Stoker, R.N.

Jennison, R. B., 40-44, N.A.2., R.N.V.R.

Johnson, G. E., 30-38, Sergeant, R.A.F., killed in action.

Jopling, J. T., 32-34, Flight Sergt., R.A.F.,
killed in action.

Kelly, H. W., 36-38, Corporal, R.E.M.E.

Kent, R. G., 25-27, Major, I.A.O.C.

Kerr-Smith, M. W., 30-34, Captain, R.A.,
Mentioned in Despatches.

Kidd, E. H., 25-28, Captain, Green Howards,
ex prisoner of war.

King, I. S., 37-41, L-MM., R.M.

King, J. M., 32-38, A/P.O., Fleet Air Arm.

King, J. W., 32-40, Flight Lieut., R.A.F., D.F.C.,
D.F.M., ex prisoner of war.

King, L. V., 34-38, Pilot Officer, R.A.F.,
killed in action.

Kirtley, R. B., 36-44, Signalman, Royal Signals.

Kirtley, R. W., 34-40, Ldg. Telegraphist, R.N.
Knowles, C. R., 34-37, Sergeant, R.A.F.

Lamb, J., 27-28, Major, R.A.
Lamb, T., 27-28, Lieut., Black Watch.
Lambert, T. M., 28-35, Lieut., R.N.V.R.
Lambert, W. B., 18-21, L.A.C., R.A.F.
Lattimer, R. J., 39-40, Lieut., R.A.I.S.E.
Lawson, F. E., 21-24, Flight Sergeant, R.A.F., killed in action.
Lawson, H. A., 28-30, Gunner Svr., R.A.
Lawson, J. E., 31-35, Sergeant, Royal Signals.
Lawson, W. F., 17-21, Corporal, C.M.P.
Little, S. W., 30-35, Sergeant, R.A.
Lockwood, B., 24-28, Sergeant, R.A.F.
Lovell, J. D., 34-38, Corporal, Royal Signals.
Lyne, W. E., 38-39, Pilot Officer, R.A.F.

Madderson, P. F., 31-35, Sergeant, R.A.F.
Markham, F. W., 31-32, Signalman, Royal Signals.
Marshall, K. H., 30-34, Flight Sergeant, R.A.F.
Mason, T. A., 35-39, Sgt. Pilot, R.A.F.
Mawson, A., 31-35, Corporal, R.A.F., died on active service.
McGregor, J. S. E. R-R., 29-33, Lieut., R.A.
McGuinness, D. E., 12-16, Chief Engineer, R.N.
McKay, C. N., 25-30, Flight Sergeant, R.A.F.
McLean, J. M., 31-37, Bdr., R.A.
Mercer, R. B., 32-35, Gunner, R.A.
Metcalfe, R., 34-38, Gunner, R.A., Discharged—wounds.
Metcalfe, W., 41-43, Sapper, R.E.
Minns, N. E., 33-36, Lieut., R.E.
Minns, R. E., 36-39, Flight Lieut., R.A.F.
Molyneux, B. D., 29-32, Sergeant, R.A.F.
Morton, A. H., 30-34, Sergeant, R.A.F.
Morton, G., 37-41, Trooper, R.A.C.

Morton, K. W., 30-32, Sergeant, R.A.F.,
killed in action.
Mosley, R. R., 30-35, Flight Sergeant, R.A.F.

Newton, A. E., 29-32, Chief Officer, Merchant Navy.
Newton, D. O., 29-32, Corporal, R.A.F.
Newton, R. C., 29-34, Flight Sergeant, R.A.F.
Newton, T. C., 29-30, Flight Lieut.,
Royal Canadian Air Force.
Nichols, O. T., 29-33.
Nicholson, H. L., 33-38, S.B.P.O.(D.C.), R.N.
Nicholson, W., 37-44, Cadet, R.A.F.

Orbinski, R. M., 30-31, Cpl., K.S.L.I.
Ottley, J. F. H. C., 34-39, Lieut., R.E.

Parnaby, D. A., 36-42, Pte., G.S.C.
Pardoe, H., 34-37, L.A.C., R.A.F.
Parker, H., 28-31, Bdr., R.A.
Pawson, W. P., 33-37, A.C., R.A.F.
Pedley, F. H., 31-38, W.O., A.E.C.
Pendlebury, M. K., 36-39, 2/Lieut., East Lancs. Regt.,
killed in action.
Pendlebury, P. J., 32-39, Lieut., R.E.
Peverill, W. T., 29-32, A.C., R.A.F.,
killed on active service.
Perrett, M., 34-36, Flying Officer, R.A.F.
Phelps, B. H., 29-34, Sergeant, R.A.F.
Pickard, E. F., 40-43, Cadet, Queen's Regt.
Plews, C. E., 16-23, Captain, R.E.
Pomeroy, F. L., 32-35, Flying Officer, R.A.F.
Porter, A.L., 35-41, A.C., R.A.F.
Porter, F. R., 36-40, Craftsman, R.E.M.E.
Proom, H., 35-39, O/S., R.N.
Proom, J. E., 26-33, Corporal, R.A.F.
Proom, W. A., 27-32, Capt., R.E.M.E.
Prosser, J. V., 33-42, Flying Officer, R.A.F.
Pybus, F. C., 25-27, Lieut., R.E.

Raw, G., 22-26, Corporal, R.A.F.
Read, G. J., 36-40, Flight Sergeant, R.A.F.
Ride, R., 29-32, L.A.C., R.A.F.
Roberts, J. D.,, 22-25, Signalman, Royal Signals,
discharged (ill health).
Robins, W. A., 22-26, Sergeant, R.A.F.
Robinson, C., 28-32, Lieut., R.N.V.R.
Robinson, C. R., 29-36, Major, R.A.
Robinson, J. M., 38-43, A.B., R.N.
Robinson, L. J.,38-39, L/Corporal, R.A.O.C.
Robinson, R. L., 30-33, Petty Officer, R.N.
Robson, J. B., 31-34, Flying Officer, R.A.F.
Rodber, E. H., 20-28, Corporal, R.A.F.
Rossor, H. B., 35-37, S.Q.M.S., R.A.O.C.
Rossor, J. G., 35-39, Craftsman, R.E.M.E.
Russell, J. H. E., 26-34, Reg. Petty Officer, R.N.,
Mentioned in Despatches.
Russill, A. W. J., 36-40, Sergeant, R.A.F.
Rutter, P. L., 35-40, L/Corporal, Highland L.I.

Sanderson, J. W., 34-40, Lieut., R. Northumberland Fus.
Sandison, H. J. V., 09-13, Commander (S), R.N.
Scarr, A. H., 38-43, S.K.R.I., R.N.
Scott, L., 33-35, Trooper, R.A.C., prisoner of war.
Severs, G. E., 40-41, Sub. Lieut., F.A.A.,
discharged (ill health).
Sewter, E. G., 29-32, Driver, Royal Signals,
ex prisoner of war.
Shaw, D. W., 24-29, Captain, Merchant Navy.
Shaw, H. S., 24-30, Lieut. Commander, R.N., D.S.C.
Shaw, K. R. W., 28-33, S/Sergeant, R.A.P.C.
Shaw, T. R., 33-37, Sergeant, R.A.F., D.F.M.,
killed in action.
Shute, G. E. F., M.C., 09-13, Lt.-Col., Indian Army,
killed in action.
Sidebottom, J. W., 33-37, Petty Officer, R.N.
Simpson, R. D., 32-36, A.C., R.A.F.,
discharged (ill-health).
Singleton, R. D., 31-39, Flying Officer, R.A.F.

Smith, D. B., 25-33, Captain, Royal Signals.
Smith, R. L., 35-40, Sgt. Nav., R.A.F.
Speirs, W., 14-19, Craftsman, R.E.M.E.
Spensley, J. W., 30-34, Flight Sergeant, R.A.F.
Spencer, F. G., 35-40, Corporal, D.L.I.
Spencer, P. G., 33-40, Cadet, R.A.F., killed on active service.
Spencer, R., 38-42, Miner.
Squires, P., 33-39, Sergeant, R.A.F., killed in action.
Stephenson, J. A., 18-21, Captain, R.E.
Stephenson, J. A. S., 23-25, Captain, R.A.O.C.
Stephenson, J. R., 30-37, Trooper, R.A.C., killed in action.
Stephenson, M., 39-45, Cadet, Queen's Regt.
St. John, C. A. R. L., 1930, Lieut., R.E.
Swainston, G. F., 37-43, O/S., R.N.
Swainston, P., 37-42, Miner.
Swallow, E. J., 28-31, Flight Sergeant, R.A.F.
Swallow, N., 31-34, Corporal, R.A.F.
Swallow, S., 31-34, L.A.C., R.A.F.
Sweetnam, T. J., 21-25, Lieut., R.A.S.C., discharged (ill health).

Tate, J. S., 35-37, Corporal, R.A.F.
Tempest, H. N., 30-36, Private, Green Howards.
Thistlethwaite, J., 25-31, Trooper, R.A.C.
Thompson, A., 38-43, Driver, R.A.S.C.
Thornberry, F., 26-30, Corporal, R.A.S.C.
Ticehurst, J. D., 31-37, Supply Petty Officer, R.N.
Todd, W. R., 23-26, Sergeant, R.A.F.
Tress, C. W. B., 10-13, Captain, R.A., ex prisoner of war.
Trood, A. G., 19-26, First Mate, Merchant Navy.
Trott, S. W., 33-38, Corporal, R.A.F.
Twalls, T. G., 1930, Staff Sergeant, Canadian Army.
Tyerman, J., 32-37, Lieut., General List.
Tyson, E. W. (Master), 40—, Captain, R.A.

Underwood, R. D., 28-32, Corporal, R.A.S.C.

Waggett, R. W., 36-42, Corporal, R.A.F.
Walker, C., 19-22, Bdr., R.A.
Walker, S. H., 31-38, L.A.C., R.A.F.
Wallis, J. D., 38-40, Sergeant, R.A.F.
Walton, W. O., 14-17, Lt.-Col., Green Howards.
Watson, I. W. B., 32-36, Gunner, R.A.
Watson, R. M., 33-37, Pilot Officer, R.A.F., killed in action.
Weatherill, S., 38-43, Private, G.S.C.
Webster, A. F., 41-43, A.C., R.A.F.
Wenham, L. P., 20-30, Lieut., R.A.O.C.
Wetherell, J. R., 09-17, Lt.-Col., R.E.
Whittingham, F., 34-40, Lieut., Yorks. and Lancs. Regt.
Wilkin, H. L., 30-37, W.O., R.A.O.C.
Williams, P. C., 34-40, Flying Officer, R.A.F., Mentioned in Despatches.
Williamson, H., 39-43, L/Corporal, Green Howards.
Willson, H. N. D., 29-32, Private, Oxford & Bucks. L.I.
Willis, F., 18-22, Corporal, R.A.F.
Wilson, N., 26-28, Squadron Leader, R.A.F., O.B.E., Mentioned in Despatches.
Wilson, W. E., 31-37, Gunner, R.A., ex-prisoner of war.
Wood, A. J. H., 35-42, Pilot Officer, R.A.F.
Wood, D. C. B., 33-36, Sergeant, R.A.S.C.
Wood, V. M., 37-41, Miner.
Woodham, A. C., 34-36, Petty Officer, R.N.
Woodham, R. B., 32-35, Rifleman, K.R.R., ex-prisoner of war.
Woodmass, J. T., 16-19, Squadron Leader, R.A.F.
Woolass, G. L., 33-37, Captain, Yorks. & Lancs. Regt.
Worrall, C. C. H. (Master), 35—, Major, D.L.I.
Worswick, A., 20-28, Sergeant, R.A.F.
Wylam, J. H., 31-37, Captain, R.E.
York, F. L., 29-33, Sgmn., Royal Signals.

Bibliography

'We Landed By Moonlight' By Group Captain Hugh Verity. DSO DFC. Published by Crecy Publishing 1995.

'Wings of Night' by Alexander Hamilton published by Crecy Books.1993

'And The Walls Came Tumbling Down' by Jack Fishman Souvenir Press 1982

The Bomber Command War Diaries by Martin Middlebrook and Chris Everitt published by Viking and Penguin Books 1985 and 1990.

The Bomber Command Losses editions 1939-40,1941 by W.R.Chorley published by Midlands County Publications 1992.

Public Record Office. Air/27/28 and all relevant 540 Operational Record Books.

Compostellan. Richmond Grammar School Magazine.

Le Currier Picard. France

Retired fire-fighter Tony Eaton is a keen amateur military historian of WW1 and WW11. He has had several articles on the Great War published in local newspapers and his latest book **'From the Dales to Jericho'** is his third book. He has previously co-authored two books on the Second World War (Ditto publishing) and both are stories of men who served with Bomber Command.

The first book **'I'm Lucky-I Believe'** is about retired Northallerton policeman Jack Bosomworth who served as a Wireless Operator/Air Gunner with No 57 (Lancaster) Squadron during the winter of 1943-44. He sorties included eight raids to Berlin and the infamous Leipzig and Nuremberg raids of February and March 1944. He completed twenty eight bombing sorties.

The second book, **'We Sat Alone'** is about Fred Whitfield DFM of South Shields who served as a Rear Gunner with No IX (Lancaster) Squadron who succeeded in shooting down 3 ½ German fighters within his first six sorties. He was on the famous Tirpitz raid in the Scandinavian Fjords and also bombed Hitler's 'Eagles Nest' at Berchtasgaten and completed forty eight bombing sorties.